DATE DUE

Sex Errors of the Body
and Related Syndromes

Sex Errors of the Body and Related Syndromes

A Guide to Counseling Children, Adolescents, and Their Families

Second Edition

by

John Money, Ph.D.

Director
Psychohormonal Research Unit
The Johns Hopkins Hospital
Professor Emeritus of
Medical Psychology and of Pediatrics
The Johns Hopkins University
School of Medicine
Baltimore

Baltimore • London • Toronto • Sydney

Paul H. Brookes Publishing Co.
P.O. Box 10624
Baltimore, Maryland 21285-0624

Copyright © 1994 by Paul H. Brookes Publishing Co., Inc.
All rights reserved.

Typeset by Signature Typesetting & Design, Baltimore, Maryland.
Manufactured in the United States of America by
The Maple Press Company, York, Pennsylvania.

The author gratefully acknowledges his niece, Sally A. Hopkins,
who created the artwork for the book's front cover.

Permission to reprint the following quotation is gratefully acknowl-
edged:
Page 113: Quotation from Money, J. (1991). *Biographies of Gender
and Hermaphroditism in Paired Comparisons*, pp. 200–201. Amsterdam: Elsevier Science. Reprinted by permission.

Library of Congress Cataloging-in-Publication Data

Money, John, 1921–
Sex errors of the body and related syndromes : a guide to counseling children,
    adolescents, and their families / by John Money. —2nd ed.
        p.   cm.
    Rev. ed. of: Sex errors of the body. c1968
    Includes bibliographical references and index.
    ISBN 1-55766-150-2 :
    1. Sex chromosome abnormalities—Patients—Counseling of. 2. Sex chro-
mosome abnormalities in children—Patients—Counseling of.
I. Money, John, 1921–   Sex errors of the body. II. Title.
[DNLM: 1. Sex Differentiation Disorders. 2. Sex Chromosome Abnormalities.
3. Sex Disorders. 4. Sex Education. WJ 712 M742s 1994]
RC881.5.M66   1994
616.6'5042—dc20
DNLM/DLC
for Library of Congress   94-14341
                                                                         CIP

British Library Cataloging-in-Publication data are available from the British
Library.

Contents

About the Author

Dr. John Money serves as Director of the Psychohormonal Research Unit at The Johns Hopkins Hospital, a unit he founded, and is Professor Emeritus of Medical Psychology and of Pediatrics at The Johns Hopkins University School of Medicine.

Dr. Money is recognized internationally for his work in psychoendocrinology and the new and growing science of developmental sexology. He introduced the now universally accepted idea that several criteria of sex exist, including genetic sex, morphologic sex, and sex role as male or female. He has a worldwide reputation in gender science, research, and clinical care, where his expertise ranges from neonatal sex assignment with sex organ irregularity or ambiguity to adult sex reassignment in transsexualism.

Dr. Money has written, coauthored, or edited more than 30 books and published hundreds of scholarly articles. His research has significantly increased the body of knowledge concerning sexual development, and his counseling has benefited thousands of individuals with sexological syndromes.

Foreword to the Second Edition

Normalcy, like sex, is a basic human need. It reminds us that life, insecure as it is, follows certain rules.

Normalcy in sex is a basic human demand. Male and female created He them. Is it a boy or a girl? Never is it an it. We tend to take normalcy for granted. It is, after all, the norm. But it also serves to reassure us of the predictability and continuity of our existence. Perhaps this is why we react so badly when our expectations of normalcy fail to be fulfilled.

This is particularly true where sex errors of the body are concerned. Even 30 years of sexual revolution have done little to demystify sex and sexuality. The mass media continue to present us with romanticized images of true love, disease-free intercourse, and anatomical correctness. Children continue to acquire most of their information from their peers. Their fantasies are still fed by the unknown, and the old taboos remain largely intact. Although public awareness and acceptance of some of the more visible and vocal minorities, such as homosexuals and transsexuals, have certainly greatly improved, even in this "enlightened" day and age a young adolescent will think more than twice before openly admitting homosexual desires.

Perhaps the most traumatic failure to meet our expectations of normalcy is presented by sex errors of the body. Genital abnormalities, in particular, challenge the basic tenets of our identities as men or women. We regard the sex we are as an eternal verity. It lies at the core of our being and is therefore sacrosanct. One of the great mysteries of creation, it is not to be tampered with, explored, analyzed, explained, or questioned. To do so is to debase it. This mystification of sex leaves no room for doubt, no place for ambiguity. The first thing asked of every new human being is whether it is a boy or a girl. It must be one or the other. There are no additional categories.

This is an attitude fraught with value judgments. This attitude causes those with "mistakes of nature" to question their self-worth. It drives their parents into agonies of guilty self-recrimination. Yet, this attitude also can prohibit intervention, medical or otherwise, to remedy the condition. We all have difficulty discussing our private parts, and sex errors are not viewed dispassionately, as simple physiological anomalies. Rather, sex errors can too often be seen as twists of fate, divine judgments, and shameful secrets to be hidden and borne in silent suffering. As such, they become a source of abuse, shame, and misunderstanding. To share such a secret is to invite ridicule and rejection; to keep such a secret condemns one to a life of loneliness and isolation. This is the dilemma of the individual with a sex error of the body.

Even professionals are poorly equipped to deal with this dilemma. Textbooks of endocrinology and gynecology contain all the technical details, but doctors receive no training in dealing with the *people* with these conditions. Furthermore, psychologists and counselors have almost no understanding of the physiological aspects of these conditions.

John Money combines expert knowledge of the medical and technical aspects with the personal experience and psychological savvy to present the total subject in a comprehensible and effective manner. Professionally engaged in this field since 1949, he is a keen and sympathetic observer of life and an expert in the "anthropology of the street corner." He knows how people live and think, and he also understands that they are not always kind and generous to those who are "different."

The great virtue of this book is that it offers clear, usable strategies to all involved in dealing with the problems of sex errors: clients, patients, parents, and counselors, but also, equally, teachers, faculty members, physicians, and other specialists. Even highly qualified experts often know little about providing proper guidance for an individual with a sex error of the body.

Money discusses anatomical as well as functional errors. The former include errors of physical development such as congenital defects in male/female differentiation, problems of puberty, and gynecomastia and hirsutism. Functional errors have to do with atypical lovemaps and gender dysphoria, as well as erectile dysfunction, premature ejaculation, penetration phobia, and the loss of sex organs.

In this book, Money shows how doctors and counselors must often begin by granting their clients "permission" to discuss subjects that are painful and taboo. He describes a highly effective parable technique for achieving this, which provides encouragement and reassurance by telling of others in similar situations and presenting the problems they encountered and how these were resolved.

Throughout history, different societies have entertained different and changing notions of sex-appropriate behavior. As the 20th century draws to a close, Western attitudes are also undergoing major readjustments. What does remain constant at all times in all places is the basic division of the human race into two sexes. A few individuals may occasionally attempt to deny even this overwhelming fact of life. Others, dissatisfied with the societal sex roles assigned to them, may rightfully try to make changes. Nevertheless, every society continues to be composed of men and women, however they dress or behave.

The issues raised in this book therefore transcend national and cultural boundaries. They are as relevant to Europe and the rest of the world as they are to the United States. The coping strategies presented may vary slightly in detail from society to society, but the principles are universally applicable.

Of course, some will argue that there is no need for a book like this at all. These people agree with the social constructionists, who maintain that our concepts of man and woman are fictions dreamed up to keep everyone comfortably in their prescribed place. They may even believe that doctors who wish to treat these "errors" are participating in a conspiracy of the medical establishment to reinforce conservative notions of normalcy and deny individuals their rightful liberation from restrictive, socially dictated role models. However, this glib assertion ignores the very real pain and suffering experienced by individuals with sexual anomalies. It is rather like the wealthy airily proclaiming that money does not buy happiness, or the physically able cheerfully enthusing that life in a wheelchair can really be quite splendid.

We all have a need to feel normal. We all need to feel that others are normal. Nowhere is this need so strong, or so laden with emotion, as in the area of sex. Is it an "it"? No parent asks this question, but all fear the answer.

Louis Gooren, M.D.
Professor of Transsexology
Free University Hospital
Amsterdam, The Netherlands

Preface to the Second Edition

When the first edition of this book appeared in 1968, it addressed the issue of sex education in the spirit of emancipation from sexually transmitted disease and inadvertent pregnancy that eventually became epitomized as a sexual revolution, better named as a sexual reformation. By the end of the 1970s, the reactionary forces of counterreformation had mobilized and were on the offensive. In 1981, a new disease was first recognized, eventually to become known as HIV/AIDS (human immunodeficiency virus/acquired immune deficiency syndrome). HIV/AIDS is a killer disease, transmitted by the exchange of bodily fluids, including sexual fluids and blood in even minute traces. HIV/AIDS has completely changed the face of sexual emancipation by equating sex with death, an equation that the population at large has not yet sufficiently assimilated so as to change its policy of whistling in the dark as it passes the graveyard.

The spirit of sexual emancipation, even though it has become much more intimidating, has not yet been extinguished. People in general are less taboo-ridden in their curiosity about sex and sexology than they were 25 years ago; witness the formerly forbidden subjects that are now aired routinely on television talk shows.

The second edition of this book has been revised to satisfy the legitimate sexological curiosity of serious people, but more particularly the curiosity of sexological scholars and therapists, and most of all to answer the questions of parents of newborns with a sex error of the body. As the babies themselves grow from childhood through adolescence to adulthood, it answers their questions too.

Words can wound. Medicine can be very cruel in using diagnostic terms as gruesome as bird-faced dwarfism and prune-belly syndrome. That is why much serious thought went into the decision to continue using *Sex Errors* in the title of this second revised and enlarged edition. Medical terms such as hermaphroditism or intersex are too stigmatizing for people born with a syndrome that affects the sex organs. They find it stigmatizing also to have to talk about themselves as having an abnormality, anomaly, defect, deviance, deficiency, disability, or handicap. They would rather use the term *sex error*. It implicates their anatomy, not themselves. For 25 years it has been evident that they are able to talk about a sex error with their parents, health care professionals, and close friends without feeling stigmatized. They do not have to hide their own copy of *Sex Errors of the Body* because of its title. Not only in its title but also in its contents the book provides people, singly or in groups, with terminology that does not do harm, but helps to prevent or heal the injury of discovery and disclosure.

Preface to the
First Edition

History sometimes dictates her own timetable for the affairs of men. Thus, it has not been until the decade of the sixties that society has been made ready to plan and discuss the sex education of its children and youth as a community responsibility. In the past, the need was not lacking—only its fulfillment. Now it seems destined that the sixties will be remembered as, among other things, the decade when sex education finally became liberalized and widely available. This greater availability of sexual information is part of a more extensive change in sexual mores which is often thought of as a sexual revolution in reaction to the taboos and prudery of Victorianism. The sexual revolution is, however, part of a tide of history that has been running for a longer period of time, contemporaneously with the larger tide of social change characteristic of our civilization, at least since the Renaissance and Reformation.

The era of Reformation showed with particular vividness the clash between antithetical systems of sexual values. Puritanism and the Inquisition both represented negativism toward sex and upheld the virtues of a regulated, authoritarian, agrarian, and medieval society. Under the Inquisition, the anti-sex forces reached a climax of horror, torture, and death seldom paralleled in Western history. The great courts of the rulers of Europe represented an attitude of tolerance toward sex with a degree of personal freedom, even licentiousness, that was predicated on social privilege and wealth—the wealth to support one's activities and maybe one's partners and offspring. The customs of the aristocracy prestigiously set the fashion for the less privileged to aspire toward. It was to be some time, however, after the fall of aristocratic privilege during the French Revolution, before aristocratic ideals of sexual freedom could be put into practice by the common man. Meantime, there would be the ambivalent era of the two-faced nineteenth century in which Puritanism and prudery vied with pornography and genteel vice—much as prohibition vies with bootlegging in parts of the South in the U.S. today.

The ambivalence of the nineteenth century persisted into the twentieth and might have continued in a state of equilibrium, except that the industrial revolution was to make its contribution to sex which would, in effect, initiate the contraceptive revolution—the perfection of a cheap, widely distributed, and erotically satisfactory contraceptive: the rubber condom. There had been crude forms of contraception before, but the latex process for manufacturing the thin rubber sheath belongs to the 1920s.

It took from early in the century until after World War II before the public faced its responsibility of providing itself with superhighways on which to run the automobiles that its industry was producing. The time lag in deciding how to use contraceptives, today more varied than in the twenties and made even more effective with the Pill, is roughly comparable.

In the flapper age of the 1920s, birth control was for the upper classes and the educated. Their sons and daughters began revising their sexual customs to include contraceptively safe sexual relations outside marriage. As a matter of public and legal policy, society was completely at odds with itself over whether it would accept birth control, even in marriage. People themselves made up society's mind for it. Married and unmarried alike, they went on practicing birth control, tasting some of that personal freedom in sexual decisions that had once been a privilege of the aristocratic and wealthy.

Personal freedom in sex is not the same as promiscuity. The postwar teenaged generation established this principle very clearly when its response to the contraceptive revolution was to invent the social institution of going steady. Today in the sixties, there is less rigidity about the obligation of getting engaged and married to the person with whom one is going steady. It is more acceptable to go steady for only as long as the bond of affection and sex keeps both partners together. The old moral values, including the double standard, have by no means disappeared. Nonetheless, the generation of the sexual revolution is quietly redefining for all adolescents, not only the aristocratic and wealthy, a new moral standard of personal freedom in sex in the era of universal contraception and population control.

Personal freedom in sex requires knowledge. Without knowledge, one can all too easily become trapped, unnecessarily and unwittingly, by remediable defects or faults in oneself or one's relationships. Knowledge requires teachers. Teachers require books—for which reason this book has been written. It is directed not only to the specialist, but also to the reader who is a layman in the field of sex and has a responsible interest in the subject. The interest may be self-interest. In that case, there will be only a few readers with problems which they can identify between these covers. Nonetheless, by learning the extremes of what can happen in the morphology and function of sex, they will enhance their appreciation of their own normalcy.

The reader who is engaged professionally in sex education and counseling, whether he be school teacher, doctor, pastor, social worker, psychologist, marriage counselor, or whatever, will find his effectiveness greatly increased by knowing of the disorders discussed herein, as sooner or later he will come across some of them in real life. They are not exceptionally rare. He will come across other sexual disorders also, notably the psychosexual disorders. They constitute the material for a companion volume not yet written.

Acknowledgments

The author has been supported in research for 37 years by the National Institute of Child Health and Human Development, Department of Health and Human Services, United States Public Health Service, currently under Grant No. 5 R25 HD00325-37.

Sally A. Hopkins and William P. Wang worked industriously on the manuscript of this book.

To the Memory of
Ruth Mary Money,
for the Generation Leaving,
and to the Memory of
David Childs Walker,
for the Generation Ahead

first edition

To the memory of
Lawson Wilkins, M.D.,
father of pediatric endocrinology

Lawson Wilkins (1894–1963) was a very pragmatic, chart-making investigator. Although not much given to psychologizing, he had the prescience to recognize that the mental and behavioral changes made possible by treatment with hormones was of very basic importance to the principles of psychology. One such treatment, discovered in 1950, was the newly synthesized hormone cortisol. This hormone made it possible to suppress from babyhood onward the virilization of girls and women with a birth defect of the sex organs (female hermaphroditism) and the endocrine syndrome of congenital adrenal hyperplasia (CAH). Within as few as 6 months, this new treatment made it possible for a heavily masculinized CAH woman to grow breasts and have her first menstrual period. Such a rapid turnaround might require the services of a psychoendocrinologist. It also provided a unique opportunity to gain new psychoendocrine knowledge. This was the context in which Wilkins, the world's first pediatric endocrinologist, invited me to join his clinic as the first pediatric psychoendocrinologist. Forty-three years later, this book is one outcome of his foresight.

second edition

Sex Errors of the Body and Related Syndromes

1

Verities and Variables of Sex

As hunters or farmers in bygone times, human beings may not have known about fish that change their sex from male to female or from female to male, nor about earthworms and other creatures that have both male and female reproductive organs. They did, however, know that wild and domesticated animals were, like themselves, either male or female. For us human beings, the division into two sexes (from the Latin *secare,* to cut or to divide) is one of the great eternal verities. The difference between the sexes has been assumed to be more impressive than the similarity, and it has been embedded as an eternal verity in the great creation myths of people everywhere.

The great creation myths may also include, however, a reference to a combined or in-between sex. It is found, somewhat concealed, in the book of Genesis where it is written that man and woman were made in God's own image, thus implying that in God the two sexes were united as one.

In ancient Greece and Rome, sculptors and potters made statues of Hermaphroditus, who represented the in-between sex, as a youthful male with well-developed breasts (Figure 1). In medical terminology, such a person would be known as an adolescent boy with gynecomastia, not as a hermaphrodite. The term hermaphrodite is correctly applied when the sex of an individual cannot be declared on the basis of the appearance of the reproductive anatomy alone. Indecision arises particularly in the case of a newborn when the external sex organs are malformed and neither fully male nor fully female in appearance.

1

Figure 1. Roman statue of reposing Hermaphroditus, the son of Hermes and Aphrodite, represented as a male youth with breasts. (Erich Lessing/Art Resource, NY.)

For centuries, farmers have known of one type of hermaphroditism that is common in cattle, namely, the freemartin. The affected calf is always twinborn with a male, is a partially masculinized female, and is predictably sterile. The diagnosis and prognosis can be made with confidence, for farmers have known about freemartins for generations, and there is no other similar condition with which to confuse it.

In human beings it is a different story, for only in a very isolated and inbred community is it possible that every newborn case of hermaphroditism will have the same diagnosis and prognosis and the same hereditary origin. After encountering several cases of the condition for two or more generations, the community learns what to expect as the infant grows up through the age of puberty. This is indeed what happened in an isolated mountain community in the Dominican Republic (Imperato-McGinley, Guerrero, Gautier, & Peterson, 1974; Imperato-McGinley, Peterson, Gautier, & Sturla, 1979). When hermaphroditism first appeared in the children of interrelated families in that community, they were assigned as girls because the babies' sex organs appeared to be female. When they reached the age of puberty, however, instead of growing breasts and feminizing, they developed more like boys or eunuchs. They were therefore unmarriageable and a financial burden on their parents. The community learned its lesson so that subsequent babies born with the condition were assigned to be reared as boys, despite the fact that their genital appearance was not male. From infancy onward, they were teased as *guevodoces,* which translates as "eggs (balls) at 12," and as *machi hembra,* which translates as "macho missy."

Far away in the eastern highlands of Papua New Guinea, in another extremely isolated and inbred community, that of the Sambia tribe, a similar hermaphroditic pedigree has been discovered (Herdt & Davidson, 1988). This hermaphroditism has the same hereditary origin, the same diagnosis (5α-reductase deficiency in chromosomal males), and the same developmental prognosis as that of the hermaphroditism in the Dominican Republic. The assignment of the baby at birth traditionally depended on whether the woman who assisted at delivery was knowledgeable enough to examine a female-appearing baby's genitals very closely. If even a slight malformation was observed, she would declare the baby to be a *kwolu-aatmwol* (hermaphrodite), for which the Pidgin term is *turnim-man,* signifying that at puberty the child would turn more into a man than a woman. Therefore, the baby would be reared as a boy. In the absence of a close genital examination, however, a hermaphroditic baby would be declared to be a girl.

As a girl, the hermaphrodite's anomaly remained concealed until she failed to feminize at puberty. This failure might be kept hidden until it was discovered at marriage by the husband, who would disavow the marriage.

As a boy, although he had no visible penis and was much teased, a hermaphrodite was permitted by the elders to go through the early phases of initiation into warriorhood, but not to graduate. The only role for him in village life might be as a shaman, or spirit doctor. The alternative was to escape to the modern urban life of a coastal city.

Isolated and genetically inbred communities are the exception, not the rule. In most places on earth, the gene pool is so mixed that when a hermaphroditic baby is born it is not possible to identify its diagnosis and prognosis by looking at it, even if its etiology is hereditary, which is not always the case. Male and female hermaphrodites may have the same genital appearance.

In the 16th century, the renowned jurist Lord Coke declared that by the common law of England "a hermaphrodite may be either male or female, and it shall succeed according to the kind of sex that doth prevail." Succession to hereditary wealth or title was the concern. The "kind of sex that prevailed" was that of adulthood, not necessarily that present at birth. Lord Coke, however, did not specify the criteria by which to judge the prevailing sex.

The vexing question of the criteria by which to determine the sex of a newborn hermaphrodite remained unresolved until the German pathologist Edwin Klebs in 1876 formulated a classifactory system of hermaphroditism based on gonadal structures. He recognized three types of hermaphrodite. True hermaphrodites possessed ovarian and testicular tissue. The other two types Klebs called pseudohermaphrodites. Male pseudohermaphrodites possessed only testicular tissue, and female pseudohermaphrodites possessed only ovarian tissue. This threefold classification is still in use. In effect, Klebs set up the ovaries and the testicles as the only criterion of sex. Of course, he wrote in an era before the discovery of hormones and before chromosomes or genes had been observed. Thus he lacked the concepts of hormonal sex and chromosomal (genetic) sex that contribute to the contemporary understanding of hermaphroditism.

As first published in 1955 by Money (1986b), the breakdown of the single male/female criterion of sex into several component variables was a direct outcome of the study of hermaphrodites. This more complex understanding of sexual differentiation is now universally recognized, and has entered the medical dictionary (Dorland's, 1981).

In the first edition of this work, *Sex Errors of the Body* (1968), I wrote of the

> sequence of developmental steps, the orderly progression of which is prerequisite to normal sexual functioning. In normal development, each step follows the other in such logical progression that one does not think of them as possibly being independent of one another. It was only through the study of sexual anomalies, such as I have paid attention to since 1951, in which the sequence of development is not as expected, that it became possible to differentiate one step from another and to identify the developmental variables of sex, which may be independent of one another. One may list these variables as follows:
>
> 1. Genetic or chromosomal sex
> 2. Gonadal sex
> 3. Fetal hormonal sex
> 4. Internal morphologic sex
> 5. External morphologic sex
> 6. Hypothalamic sex
> 7. Sex of assignment and rearing
> 8. Pubertal hormonal sex
> 9. Gender identity and role
> 10. Procreative sex impairments
>
> Each of these variables of development has its own probabilities of error or malfunction. Some of the errors overlap from one variable to another. One does not say that an anomaly is caused by a particular variable, because the cause is actually much more complicated than that and usually is a chain of events. Thus, a genetic error may lead to an error in

the production of fetal hormones or an error in their use, which in turn leads to an error of sex-organ morphology, and so forth. For this reason, the principle of classification in what follows is a temporal and not a causal one. (pp. 11–12)

The concept of multiple components that are influential sequentially over time is summarized diagrammatically in Figure 2, which begins

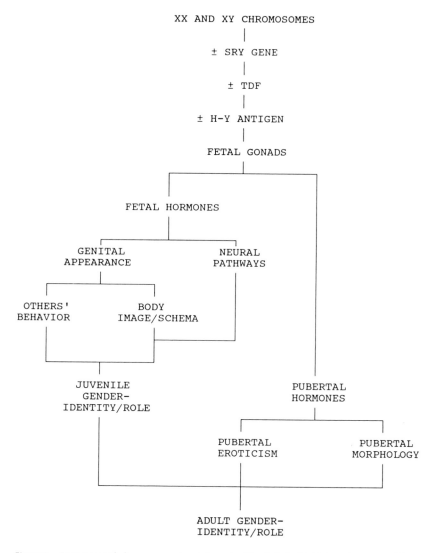

Figure 2.   From prenatal chromosomes to adult gender-identity/role: Multiple and sequential determinants. SRY=Sex-determining Region of Y chromosome; TDF=Testis-Determining Factor.

with chromosomes and carries through to the establishment of gender-identity/role (G-I/R).

Taking into account many components and factoring in a time variable makes possible the formulation of the proposition **nature/critical period/nurture** in place of the outworn proposition, **nature/nurture.** The critical period signifies that the interaction of nature and nurture together advances development, but only if that interaction takes place at the critical period, neither too soon nor too late, but precisely on time. Then, once the critical period passes, there is no backtracking. The outcome is fixed and immutable.

The outmoded nature/nurture debate dies a lingering death. In fact, it took a new lease on life when in the 1970s nurturists first became "labeling theorists" and later, "social constructionists." They align themselves against biology and medicine, which they condemn as essentialist and incompatible with social constructionist theory. They consider all sex differences as artifacts of social construction. In cases of birth defects of the sex organs, they attack all medical and surgical interventions as unjustified meddling designed to force babies into fixed social molds of male and female, instead of allowing them to be a medically unmolested third sex. One writer has gone even to the extreme of proposing that there are five sexes, namely Klebs's three varieties of hermaphrodite, as well as ordinary males and females (Fausto-Sterling, 1993).

Without medical intervention, the fate of many hermaphroditic babies is to die. Before contemporary medical interventions, many children with a birth defect of the sex organs were condemned to grow up as they were born, stigmatized and traumatized. It simply does not make sense to talk of a third sex, or of a fourth or fifth, when the phylogenetic scheme of things is two sexes. Those who are genitally neither male nor female but incomplete are not a third sex. They are a mixed sex or an in-between sex. To advocate medical nonintervention is irresponsible. It runs counter to everything that this book stands for, which is to enhance health and well-being to the greatest extent possible.

2

Sex-Chromosome Anomalies

As soon as the egg from the mother's ovary and the sperm from the father's testicle join together to create a fertilized cell, it is possible by looking under a microscope at the chromosomes inside the cell to predict whether the baby of which the cell is the forerunner will be a boy or a girl. In the cell there are 46 chromosomes, 23 brought by the egg and 23 brought by the sperm (Figure 3). The egg always brings one X chromosome among the 23. The sperm brings either another X or a Y, which is much smaller. When two X chromosomes meet, the stage is set for the baby to develop as a girl (Figure 4). When an X and a Y meet, the stage is set for the baby to be a boy (Figure 5). The Y chromosome contains within its gene sequence the SRY (the Sex-determining Region on the Y) that will eventually set in motion the cascade of events that allows the cell to develop into a boy. For the cell to develop into a girl, no special sex-determining gene sequence is needed. Female differentiation and development is Nature's priority. For male differentiation and development to take place, something extra must be added. Eve first, then Adam is Nature's master plan.

It is possible for either the egg or sperm to carry too many or too few sex chromosomes or a damaged one into the cell. Alternatively, in the earliest stages of cell replication, the sex chromosomes may be unequally distributed. One way or another, it is possible for a cell to carry a sex-chromosome error without dying. If the cell lives, as it multiplies the error is copied into each of the new cells that cluster to form the embryo, and it is eventually copied into every cell of the body as the embryo develops. The signs and symptoms of having a chromosomal error in

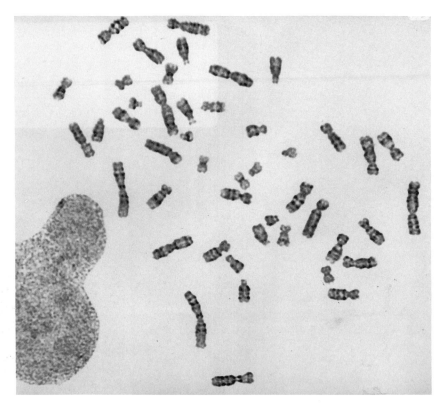

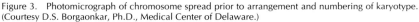

Figure 3.   Photomicrograph of chromosome spread prior to arrangement and numbering of karyotype. (Courtesy D.S. Borgaonkar, Ph.D., Medical Center of Delaware.)

every cell of every organ in the body differ from one individual to another. They may be simple or complex, mild or severe. In some cases, a sex-chromosome error may be discovered, if at all, only by chance.

None of the sex-chromosome errors were identified until development of a method (Tijo & Levan, 1956) for photographing chromosomes under a microscope and then arranging and counting them according to size and shape in a karyotype, or chromosome analysis, as shown in Figures 4 and 5.

Some genetically transmitted disorders are chromosomally sex linked (or X-linked). Most of them do not affect the sex organs or other aspects of sexual development. Examples of sex-linked disorders that do not involve sexual anomalies are fragile X syndrome, muscular dystrophy, hemophilia, and color blindness. In this work, chromosomally sex-linked disorders that result from a missing or extra chromosome are considered.

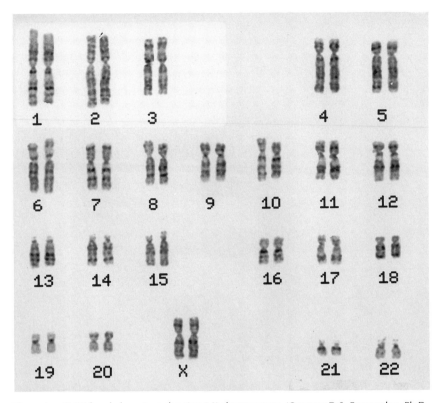

Figure 4. 46,XX female karyotype showing 2 X chromosomes. (Courtesy D.S. Borgaonkar, Ph.D., Medical Center of Delaware.)

TRIPLE X (47,XXX) SYNDROME

In the cells of girls and women with triple X syndrome (Figure 6), there is an extra or supernumerary X chromosome. The total chromosome count is 47,XXX instead of 46,XX. In some individuals, there may be two or even three supernumerary X chromosomes. The more extra X chromosomes, the more intelligence is likely to be impaired. The proportion of individuals with triple X syndrome is higher among people with mental retardation than in the general population. The frequency of 47,XXX syndrome in the general population has not been accurately ascertained. Many cases pass unnoticed as the girls and women have no physical or mental symptoms to bring them to medical attention. They work, marry, and perhaps bear children if fertility is not affected, unaware of the extra chromosome in their cells.

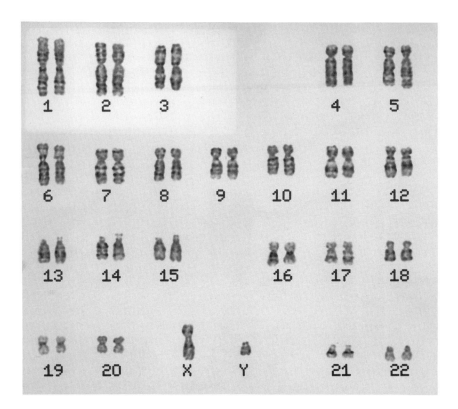

Figure 5. 46,XY male karyotype showing X and Y chromosomes. (Courtesy D.S. Borgaonkar, Ph.D., Medical Center of Delaware.)

SUPERNUMERARY Y (47,XYY) SYNDROME

In the cells of boys and men with supernumerary Y syndrome (Figure 7) there is an extra or supernumerary Y chromosome. The total chromosome count is 47,XYY instead of 46,XY. In some cases, there may be not one but two or even three extra Y chromosomes and, rarely, an extra X chromosome as well. The greater the number of extra chromosomes, the greater the number and severity of physical and mental anomalies.

Early in the history of chromosome counting, a survey of inmates in a maximum security prison in Scotland identified several individuals with supernumerary Y syndrome. The sensationalized conclusion was that the extra Y chromosome(s) increased the amount of masculine violence (Jacobs, Brinton, Melville, Brittain, & McClemont, 1965). This has proven to be a false conclusion. First, the majority of crimes committed by the XYY men in this survey were robberies and not assaults against people. Second, subsequent surveys identified XYY men and boys in the general population without a criminal history. What many males with supernumerary Y syndrome do, however, have in common is a high degree of impulsivity, which ranges from impulsive generosity to impulsive sexuality, rage, and suicide. Their impulsive behavior is exacerbated by discipline and punishment. In boyhood their behavior is manifestly problematic and capricious at home, at school, and in the community. Parents and teachers can benefit from professional counseling with respect to best intervention practices and service coordination. The extra Y chromosome is compatible with average-to-high IQ and with average-to-high achievement despite a decreased attention span and broken schooling in some instances. There are various sporadic physical anomalies, including sterility, but they are not universal. Adult height is typi-

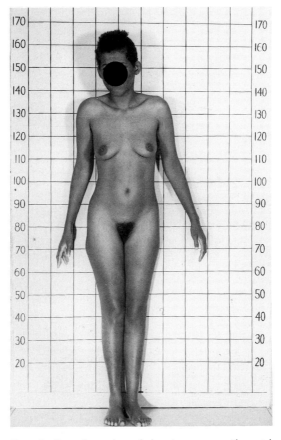

Figure 6. Normal sexual morphology in a woman with mental retardation with triple X (47,XXX) syndrome.

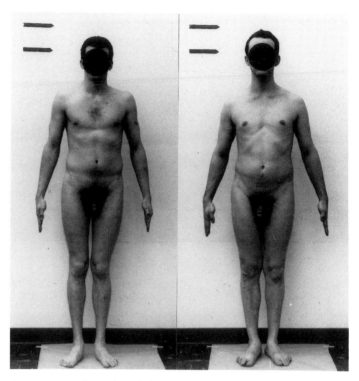

Figure 7. Normal sexual morphology in two men with supernumerary Y (47,XYY) syndrome. Heights 6'1½" and 6'2"; IQs low normal and normal; police records in both histories. (Courtesy E. Philip Welch, Dalhousie University.)

cally over 6 feet (183 cm). There are no secure data on the frequency in the general population. The figure most often quoted in textbooks is 1:1,000 male births, but it is not fixed.

KLINEFELTER (47,XXY) SYNDROME

In the cells of boys and men with Klinefelter syndrome there is an extra or supernumerary X chromosome. The total chromosome count is 47,XXY instead of 46,XY, and there may be two or three extra X chromosomes. The more X chromosomes, the higher the risk of accompanying physical and mental anomalies. The most frequently quoted figure for the incidence of 47,XXY in the general population is 1:900 male births. The prevalence of 47,XXY among males with behavior, emotional, and developmental disabilities surveyed in residential institutions may be as high as 1:500. An extra X chromosome is, however, compatible with superior IQ as well as with unimpaired mental health and law-abiding conduct, as is recognized in cases evaluated for infertility.

The XXY diagnosis is usually not made before puberty, as there are no easily recognized diagnostic clues before that time. In adolescence, swelling of the breasts (gynecomastia) as if in a girl may be a sign (Figure 8). The postpubertal body build is typically gangling, with arms and legs disproportionately long. Obesity is rare. The testicles are uncommonly small, and the spermatic tubules are unable to produce sperms. The penis also is likely to be small. Pubertal development is mostly sluggish and masculinization insufficient, but masculine normalization can be achieved by hormonal treatment with high doses of testosterone, but only if the dosage is at least double or higher than that used for males who have no testicles. Although the subjective feeling of sex drive is typically low, there are some reported incidences of sexopathological behavior disorders. Sexopathological behavior disorders and a wide variety of psychiatric and neurological pathologies occur sporadically in the 47,XXY population, and with a somewhat higher prevalence than expected in a randomly selected clinical population.

Males with 47,XXY syndrome may have difficulty with mental operations that require sequencing events in time but not with spatial percep-

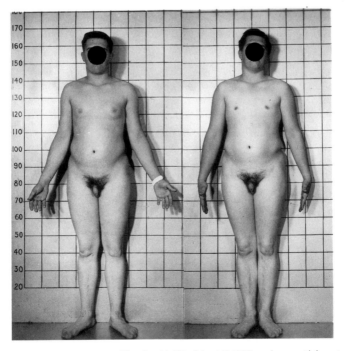

Figure 8. Nineteen-year-old male with Klinefelter (47,XXY) syndrome with breast development and hypogonadism before (left) and after (right) surgical removal of breast tissue.

tion involving rotating shapes in space. This affects language skills and reading more than calculation and practical skills. In early childhood boys with 47,XXY syndrome may need speech-language therapy.

TURNER (45,X) SYNDROME

The cells of girls and women with Turner syndrome are missing a sex chromosome. The missing chromosome could be either an X or Y chromosome. The total chromosome count is typically 45,X instead of 46,XX, but there are other possibilities. The second X chromosome may be present, but with one of its arms broken (a deletion chromosome). Alternatively, the second X chromosome may be present in some cells but not in others, thus producing a mosaic of 45,X/46,XX. (A mosaic is two genetically different types of cells in one individual.) Several other mosaics also are possible, such as 45,X/46,XX/47,XXX. The incidence of Turner syndrome has been estimated at 1:5,000 female births.

In all of these chromosomal variants, there are two defining characteristics of Turner syndrome. First, in place of ovaries there are gonadal streaks, the end product of agenesis (lack of development) or dysgenesis (abnormal development) of the ovaries (or gonads) in embryonic life. Second, short stature is the other defining characteristic. Children are brought to the clinic because of failure to grow in height. The adult height may be no more than 4 feet, 6 inches (137 cm) and is seldom more than 5 feet (152 cm).

In ways that are not yet understood, the missing X chromosome in Turner syndrome is responsible for many possible impairments of the body and its organs (Figure 9). These impairments occur sporadically, without apparent rhyme or reason, so that some females have none and others have one or more. These possible impairments include webbed neck, webbed fingers and toes, small receding chin, pigmented moles, epicanthal folds (eye folds) that resemble those of Asian peoples, blue-baby and other heart defects, kidney and ureter defects, and hearing loss. In cognitive function there may be an impairment of nonverbal (praxic) intelligence, calculation, direction sense, and motor coordination, all of which affect school achievement.

Lacking ovaries to make the female sex hormones, estrogen and progesterone, teen-age girls with Turner syndrome need to take these hormones by mouth. In adulthood the necessary dosage of these hormones is equivalent to that found in birth control pills, which can, therefore, be used, possibly supplemented by a minute dose of androgen, equal to that in typical females, to energize the feeling of sexual drive. The hormones are taken cyclically, 3 weeks on and 1 week off, in order to follow the normal menstrual cycle and allow menstruation to occur.

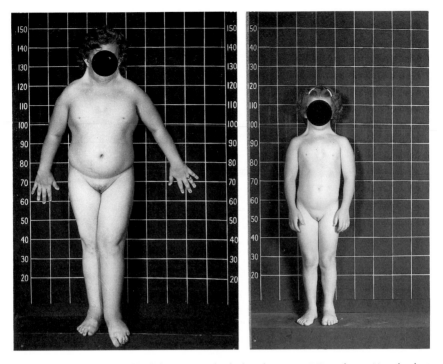

Figure 9. Varying degrees of disability in two individuals with Turner (45,X) syndrome. Note the short stature in both and the sexual infantilism in the older girl (left) at age 15. The younger girl (right) is 10½ years of age.

In girls with Turner syndrome, the time for commencing hormone treatment to bring about pubertal feminization (Figure 10) is a compromise between height age, chronological age, and social age. The decision is made with the help of counseling. It may be advisable for girls who are very short to hold off hormonal therapy until age 15, or even later. In the meantime, treatment with a synthetic growth hormone or a growth-promoting synthetic anabolic steroidal hormone such as oxandrolone or fluoxymesterone may, but is not guaranteed, to promote a slight addition to ultimate adult height.

Because they have uteri, girls with Turner syndrome are able to have menstrual periods after receiving hormonal treatment. With appropriate intervention, they are able to become pregnant, despite the absence of ovaries and eggs. The pregnancy begins *in vitro* (literally, in a glass dish) in a fertility laboratory where sperms are mixed with an egg donated from another woman's ovary. One sperm cell from among millions and the single egg cell unite to form a fertilized cell which, after multiplying a few times, is transplanted into the woman's uterus. There the fertilized cell takes hold and grows into a baby.

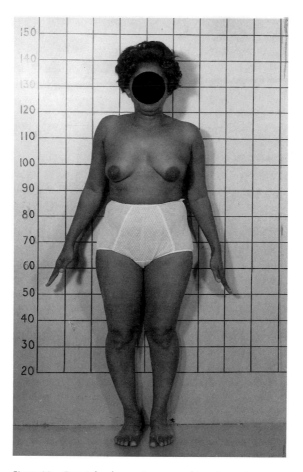

Figure 10.   Breast development as a sequel to estrogen treatment, beginning in teenage years, in a 28-year-old woman with Turner (45,X) syndrome.

Despite their varying disabilities, girls and women with Turner syndrome have a surprising degree of resiliency in coping with stress and adversity. In addition, they often evidence a strong history of maternalism from the days of childhood doll play onward.

Academically, prevalent difficulties among girls with Turner syndrome are reflected in a discrepancy between verbal and nonverbal IQ, the latter being lower, sometimes conspicuously so. Some girls with Turner syndrome have difficulties with directional sense and with mental operations in which shapes assume new meaning when rotated from front-to-back, sideways, or upside down. Girls with Turner syndrome do not rotate, for example, b and d, and p and q, and do not have trouble reading. By contrast, they often have difficulty with mathematics and graphic and practical skills. From kindergarten through college, they benefit from medical and academic intervention to help with any cognitive and learning difficulties they may have. They should not be penalized for low grades in mathematics, graphic arts, and physical education.

45,X/46,XY SYNDROME

Unlike the 45,X chromosome count of Turner syndrome, there is no 45,Y chromosome count, for a fertilized cell with that count is not viable. However, one of the chromosomal mosaics of Turner syndrome, 45,X/46,XX, has as its counterpart, 45,X/46,XY. Both mosaics are viable. There is some similarity between Turner syndrome and the 45,X/46,XY syndrome, with both characterized by short stature, for example, and defective or dysgenetic gonads. The outcome of gonadal dysgenesis in 45,X/46,XY may be a gonadal streak, but there also may be enough testicular tissue in the streak, typically on one side only, to supply the embryo and fetus with sufficient masculinizing hormone to allow the Adam principle to express itself, albeit imperfectly. When the baby is born, the external genitals may look like those of a male, or they may appear sexually ambiguous with a protrusion that might be called an oversized clitoris or an undersized penis without a urinary tube and with its urinary opening more or less in the female position (Figure 11).

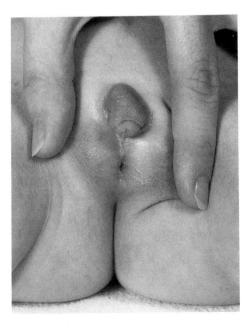

Figure 11. Congenital malformation of the genitalia in a case of 45,X/46,XY hermaphroditism with dysgenetic formation of the gonads and male sex assignment.

Neonatal announcement of the sex as boy or girl, as in all instances of sexual ambiguity, requires a careful weighing of the pros and cons of reconstructive genital surgery for a successful sex life in adulthood, the number of anticipated surgical interventions in childhood, freedom from postsurgical, especially urinary, complications in later life, hormonal management at puberty, and predicted adult height. Preservation of the defective testicular tissue with a view to fertility is not justified, for the danger of cancer is too high to warrant retention of the tissue.

3

Gonadal Anomalies

Turner and Klinefelter syndromes nicely demonstrate the relationship that may exist between an abnormal number of chromosomes and abnormal gonads, with resultant sterility. In other cases of gonadal defect, however, an abnormal chromosome count cannot be implicated, even though there may be a hereditary factor carried in the genes responsible for the gonadal defect.

In the embryo, when the primitive, undifferentiated gonad develops into an ovary, the rind or cortical part proliferates. The gonad becomes a testis if the core of the gonad develops. It is more common to find defective gonadal development in a person with the body morphology of a male than of a female. In other words, the testes are more often defective than are the ovaries. This disparity probably has something to do with Nature's embryonic priority, according to the Eve principle, to develop a female, and to add something to the basic female formula to differentiate a male. It is more complex to develop a male, and greater complexity allows a greater chance of error.

UNDESCENDED TESTES (CRYPTORCHIDISM)

The most common defect in testicular development is the failure of one or both testicles to descend. In the majority of individuals, the testicles will probably descend of their own accord either before or around the time of puberty. It is something of a medical dilemma to decide whether to not intervene or to try to induce descent early in life by means of hormonal treatment or, as a last resort, by surgery. Both approaches may fail. Some testes are destined to remain undescended, being imperfect organs from the beginning.

In a few rare instances, an empty scrotum may be a sign of other internal anomalies, for example, hermaphroditism. It is even possible for a 46,XX female with two ovaries to be so masculinized externally that the clitoris becomes a normal penis, the labia minora become the skin surrounding the penis, and the labia majora become the fused but empty scrotum (this is covered more fully in Chapter 6). When in doubt, it is wise for a child with no palpable testicles to have a diagnostic work-up, the younger the better, at a medical center equipped to perform the full range of evaluative procedures. Once is enough, however! The first time should be complete. It is too easy for a boy to have so much anxiety and attention focused on his empty scrotum that he becomes a psychosexological invalid, unnecessarily.

A few boys with an empty scrotum are found to have no testicles at all (Figure 12) or small ones that, if untreated, may eventually atrophy and disappear, perhaps due to a little-understood condition in which the body becomes self-immunized against one of its own organs. These boys

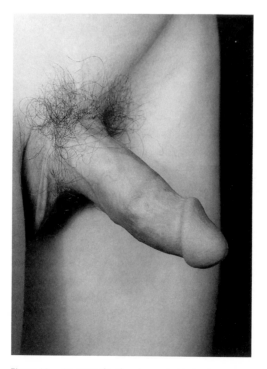

Figure 12. An example of undescended testes in a young teenager. Note the masculinizing effect of androgen on sexual hair and erectile potency.

can be given hormone replacement therapy, beginning in their early teens, so that they are developmentally indistinguishable from typical males, except for their infertility. When the testes are missing, they can be replaced with prosthetic substitutes made of silicone rubber (Figure 13). In either case, except for infertility, sexual life in adulthood can be the same as for men with descended testes of normal size.

There are two considerations to be added in counseling boys with cryptorchidism. The first is to be medically frank and to keep them well informed about diagnostic implications, proposed treatment, and prognosis. The second consideration is to make provision for them to be excused from exposing themselves in shower and locker rooms if they are embarrassed by their condition. Those who are sterile will need special counseling.

Because cryptorchidism may require a hospital admission for diagnostic purposes or surgical treatment, it is one of the many sexual anomalies, male or female, that produces a problem for a child, and the parents also, in knowing what to tell other people. A bewildered child can be greatly helped by having the appropriate explanatory word or phrase to use, especially with friends. In this case, rather than having to circulate information about undescended testes or a testicular implant, he may be more self-assured saying that his incision was to correct an internal condition, or to prevent a hernia.

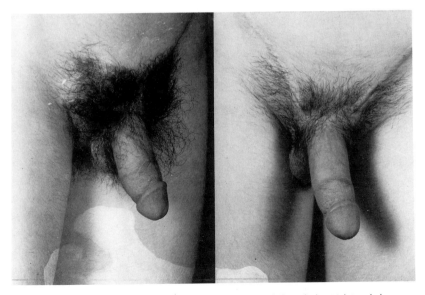

Figure 13. Congenital absence of the testes (anorchia) before (left) and after (right) male hormone (androgen) treatment and surgical implantation of silicone prosthetic testes.

SWYER SYNDROME (PURE GONADAL DYSGENESIS)

The alternative name of Swyer syndrome, pure gonadal dysgenesis, acknowledges that instead of either ovaries or testicles there are only inactive streaks of tissue similar to those found in Turner syndrome. In contrast with Turner syndrome, however, instead of a missing chromosome, there is a Y chromosome, and the count is 46,XY, which usually is a guarantee that an embryo will develop as a male. That guarantee does not hold in Swyer syndrome, and the failure may be traced to a missing segment in the genetic material of the Sex-determining Region of the Y chromosome (SRY) on the short arm of the Y chromosome. Without the SRY gene, the embryo cannot develop testicles, only inert streaks. Without testicles, the masculinizing hormones that they produce and that are essential to differentiate a male are also missing. The Adam principle fails, and by default the Eve principle takes over, and the baby differentiates as a female with no ovaries. At birth, there are no distinguishing signs of this anomaly. The child grows up as a girl. Suspicions are aroused when, at the expected age, there is no breast enlargement and no onset of menstrual bleeding, only continued increase in height, and the growth of some pubic and axillary hair.

When the diagnosis is established, typically by a gynecologist, treatment with feminizing hormones is the same as that indicated for Turner syndrome, but without the delay to gain increased height, for girls with Swyer syndrome grow tall. Pregnancy by *in vitro* fertilization with a donated egg is possible because a female with this syndrome does have a uterus. Counseling focuses chiefly on issues of infertility and induced pregnancy. Swyer syndrome is rare, but no one knows precisely how rare.

4

Fetal Hormonal Anomalies

As long ago as the remote centuries of antiquity, human beings knew about the effects of sex hormones from the testicles on sexual maturation in male animals without knowing anything whatsoever about sex hormones themselves and without having a word for them. Their knowledge came from the farm practice of gelding (castrating) young male animals. Gelded males remained sexually immature and behaviorally more docile than mature male animals. Historically, human males also have been castrated upon capture and enslavement, if destined to become functionaries in an imperial household or attendants in a harem, or to retain their male soprano role (soprano castrato) in the church choir or the opera when female singers were prohibited from public performances.

Sex hormones, like all other hormones, are highly concentrated biochemical substances. The body manufactures sex hormones chiefly in the hormone-secreting cells of the gonads, namely, the testes (testicles) of the male and the ovaries of the female. To a lesser extent, sex hormones are also secreted by the adrenocortical glands (situated above the kidneys), which also secrete cortisol, a hormone essential to the maintenance of life. In addition, during pregnancy, the placenta secretes a sex hormone, predominantly progesterone, that regulates gestation.

The sex hormones are, metaphorically speaking, all first cousins of one another. Collectively they are known as sex steroids, which signifies that they belong in the same biochemical category as oils and fats, whereas other hormones (e.g., growth hormone) are in the same category as proteins. The process by which the body manufactures sex

23

(steroidal) hormones begins with cholesterol that is transformed, in a complicated stepwise sequence, into progesterone from which is derived either cortisol or testosterone, from which is derived estrogen. From the cells in which they are manufactured, sex (steroidal) hormones are absorbed directly into the bloodstream, which delivers them throughout the body to the various organs that require them. What is not needed is filtered out by the kidneys into the urine. Thus, sex hormones can be extracted from urine, blood, or actual cells and measured. The techniques for extracting and measuring sex hormones were first developed in the 1920s. The chemical structure of these hormones was ascertained in the following decade and they were able to be synthesized in the laboratory. By the 1940s, they were marketed commercially.

The names of the sex hormones are related to their sources. Those from male sources were named, generically, male hormones or androgens (from the Greek *andros*, male). Testosterone is the male hormone derived specifically from the testes. Testosterone has many variants, some more biologically active and some more inert than others. Dihydro-testosterone, one of the active variants, is formed by the action of the enzyme 5α-reductase on testosterone.

Estrogen derives its name from the Latin *estrus*, which in animals is the period in the female sexual cycle when the animal is ovulating and in heat. Progesterone derives its name from gestation, to signify that the level of the hormone is high when the female is pregnant or gestating. This name fails to indicate, however, that in women the level of progesterone is high every month as the onset of menstruation approaches. Estrogen and progesterone together are known as female sex hormones.

One might easily assume that male sex hormones are found exclusively in males, and female sex hormones are found exclusively in females. However, this is not the case. The human sex hormones are shared by males and females. We all have some of each. The difference between sex hormones in men and women is quantitative. Men have a higher level of androgens than women do, and women have a higher level of female hormones than men do. If women had a zero level of male hormones, they would have no axillary or pubic hair. It is likely, but not absolutely proven, that without some androgen (from the ovaries and adrenocortical glands) women would experience a lack of the feeling of sexual drive or libido. A minute dose of androgen may be prescribed to enliven libido in women, especially in conjunction with female hormone replacement therapy following menopause. If men had no androgen, then the level of estrogen secreted normally by the testicles would be high enough to induce breast enlargement. A total lack of androgen would also prevent baldness in those who are genetically susceptible.

Until the 20th century, it was generally assumed that testicles and ovaries are dormant in infancy and childhood (popularized incorrectly by Freud as the latency period) until the hormonal onset of puberty and adolescence. That assumption was shattered by research in endocrinology, the branch of biomedical science that studies the endocrine glands, the glands in which hormones are produced. Developmental sexual endocrinology is the branch of science from which the Adam/Eve principle is derived. Biomedical science has shown that the testicles are hormonally extremely active during the fetal period of life and in the immediate postnatal period. If they are not properly active, or if their hormone (testosterone) does not bind to the cells that need it, then development of the male fails or is incomplete.

Masculine and feminine development begin very early in embryonic life when the internal sexual organs are neither masculine nor feminine, but both. The testicles become microscopically recognizable at the 6th week, and the ovaries at the 12th week. The other internal sexual organs are represented initially only as two pairs of microscopically small tubes or ducts. Each pair is named for the embryologist who discovered them: mullerian for the two feminine ducts, and wolffian for the two masculine ducts. The mullerian ducts obey the Eve principle and, of their own accord, differentiate into the uterus and two fallopian tubes if the baby is to be a girl. Meanwhile, the wolffian ducts wither away.

By contrast, if the baby is destined to be a boy, in obedience to the Adam principle the wolffian ducts need prodding in order to grow into the internal male reproductive structures. That prodding comes from the two hormones secreted by the tiny testicles. One hormone is androgen, the masculinizing hormone that promotes the growth of male sexual anatomy. The other is antimullerian hormone (which makes a brief appearance in embryonic life only) that instructs the mullerian ducts to wither away.

After the internal organs are formed, the external organs are in turn formed. Once again the Eve principle takes priority, so that without an additional stimulus the precursors of the external sexual anatomy develop as female. The same precursors of the external sexual anatomy develop as male in accordance with the Adam principle if they are stimulated by the male hormone, which usually comes from the fetus's own testes, but in rare cases may also be transported from the mother through the placenta. In external sexual anatomy, the penis corresponds to the clitoris, the foreskin corresponds to the clitoral hood, the skin of the penis corresponds to the labia minora, and the fused scrotum corresponds to the unfused labia majora (discussed in more detail in Chapter 6).

It is possible, experimentally in animals, to demonstrate the influence of hormones on the development of the external sexual anatomy. The Eve principle is demonstrated in male fetuses by depriving them of the male sex hormone exactly when the external organs are forming. This is done by injecting the pregnant female with a hormone that is an androgen antagonist or antiandrogen, such as cyproterone acetate, trade-named Androcur (Figures 14 and 15). The antiandrogen cancels the hormonal influence of the androgen produced by the testes of the fetus, whereupon the Eve principle takes over and the external sex organs develop as female. The same effect can be obtained by the delicate operation of castrating the animal fetus at the critical developmental period.

An experimental demonstration of the Adam principle can be achieved by implanting a pellet of the male hormone testosterone under the skin of the pregnant mother. This is timed to coincide precisely with the critical period of the formation of the external sex organs of the

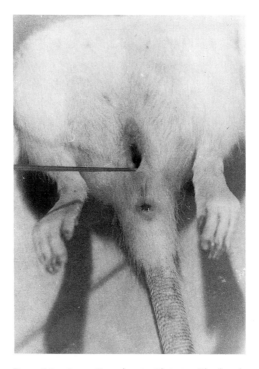

Figure 14.   A genetic male rat with testes. The female external anatomy was produced by injecting the pregnant female with an antiandrogen, cyproterone acetate, 10 mg. a day from day 12 to day 22 of pregnancy. The baby was given another 0.3 mg. of antiandrogen daily for 3 weeks after birth. (Courtesy Friedmund Neumann, Schering-Plough AG, Berlin, Germany.)

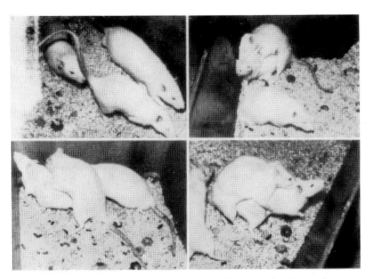

Figure 15. Mounting behavior of cyproterone-treated, feminized male rats subsequently castrated and implanted with ovarian grafts. Top left: The feminized male rat (note the
steep rising of the tail) is pursued by a normal male. Top right: Mounting attempt of the
normal male is answered with defense reaction by the feminized male. Bottom left:
Mounting attempt of the male rat is not answered with lordosis (crouching) reaction by
the feminized rat. Bottom right: Mounting attempt of the male rat is answered with lordosis reaction by the feminized male. (Courtesy F. Neumann & W. Elger, 1966
Endokrinologie, 50:221.)

daughter fetus. The male hormone is carried from the mother through
the umbilical cord, and the external sex organs are formed as they would
be for a male (Figure 16). When the experiment was performed with
sheep (Clarke, 1977; Short & Clarke, n.d.), the lamb grew up to have the
mating behavior not of a ewe but a ram and, amazingly enough, to be
treated as a ram by the normal ewes and rams in the flock.

ANDROGEN INSENSITIVITY SYNDROME (AIS)

The human anomaly that corresponds to the animal experiment with
the antiandrogen is known as androgen insensitivity syndrome (AIS),
formerly called testicular feminizing syndrome. As with Swyer syndrome, AIS demonstrates that when the Adam principle cannot operate
early in fetal life, the Eve principle takes over and directs future development as female.

Before it ceases to function, the Adam principle in AIS has its begin-
nings in a fertilized cell that bears a Y chromosome from the sperm and a
X chromosome from the egg. Ordinarily, a 46,XY fertilized cell develops
into a male. In an individual with AIS, however, the X chromosome car-

Figure 16.   A newborn genetic female monkey with ovaries. The male external anatomy was produced by injecting the pregnant mother with the male sex hormone testosterone. Arrow points to the penis, which is retracted, as is normal. (Courtesy Robert Goy & Charles Phoenix, Oregon Regional Primate Center.)

ries a defective gene that throughout prenatal and postnatal life makes it impossible for the cells in the body that require androgen to take up and use the androgen they need. The Y chromosome from the sperm does not carry a replacement for the defective gene, but an X from the sperm to match the X from the egg does. Thus a 46,XX fertilized cell may conceal the defective gene and will not develop into a girl with AIS. AIS is found exclusively in 46,XY girls and women in whom the Adam principle ceased to operate and the Eve principle took over.

Prior to the cessation of the Adam principle in an embryo with androgen insensitivity syndrome, the gonadal precursor cells form testicular structures. These testicular structures secrete the hormones testosterone and antimullerian hormone as expected. The latter succeeds in preventing the mullerian ducts from becoming female organs (uterus and fallopian tubes), as in a normal male. Testicular androgen (testosterone), however, cannot overcome the androgen resistance of the cells that should grow into male organs. Thus, the Adam principle cannot operate and the Eve principle takes over. The result is the formation of female external organs, but the vaginal canal lacks depth and ends blindly, as there are no internal female organs with which it could connect.

The Eve principle continues to operate at the time of puberty. Once again, although each cell in the body is unable to absorb androgen, it is able to absorb the lesser amount of estrogen, the feminizing hormone, that is released normally in males from testicular tissue. Thus the breasts enlarge despite the absence of ovaries, and the body shape develops as feminine (Figure 17). In the absence of a uterus, menstruation does not

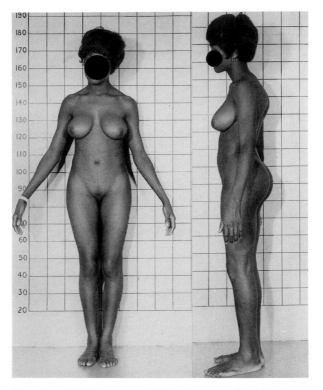

Figure 17. A 46,XY woman (technically chromosomally male with two testes) with androgen insensitivity syndrome (AIS). Note the absence of pubic hair. The gender identity and role are female. Breast growth required no treatment and was brought about by estrogen, which is normally secreted from the testes in the male.

occur. Pubic and axillary hair growth is either sparse or absent, as hair follicles in both regions are not able to respond to androgen in order to grow hair.

In many individuals with AIS, failure to menstruate is the first sign that brings them to seek medical attention. For other individuals, the diagnosis may be suspected if AIS has already been identified in a sister, aunt, or niece, for the syndrome may recur within a family. In still other individuals, AIS may be suspected when swellings are discovered in the region of the labia majora and prove to be infertile testicular masses trying to descend. Later in life, these testicular masses may be surgically removed, even if they are internal in the abdominal cavity, as a safeguard against cancer, especially if there is a family history of the disease. To promote psychological well-being in adolescence, however, they should not be removed until they have completed in full their work of pubertal feminization. After removal, female hormone replacement therapy is essential.

If the vagina is too shallow for sexual intercourse, it may be lengthened by progressive dilation or by reconstructive surgical vaginoplasty. If dilation is not anatomically feasible, surgery, known as a McIndoe procedure, is an option. However, dilation is the intervention of first choice. It is self-performed, using a progressively enlarged series of penis-shaped dilators, which may be specially constructed or obtained commercially. Gentle pressure is applied into the vaginal outlet, and over the course of several weeks, or longer, a 10-minute period of dilation twice a day may suffice.

In some cases, dilation has not proved to be a satisfactory intervention because no supportive psychosexological counseling was provided. Any girl or woman may have a genuine phobia of vaginal penetration, so that the insertion of a dilator is experienced as the traumatizing equivalent of inserting a rod into the urethra or a blunt instrument into an eye socket. In addition, in cultures that morally condemn and/or brutally punish masturbation, therapy involving a dilator may be equated with masturbation.

It is may be too traumatizing for many girls and women to have to undergo vaginal surgery or self-dilation in preparation for their first sexual encounter after, rather than before, they already have a boyfriend or husband. However, it is possible for those who begin a sex life early to experience successful penovaginal dilation if the young lover is patient and never pushes too hard.

5

Internal Organ Anomalies

When a baby's sex organs are forming during the course of prenatal development, if the Eve principle falters, it is almost always after the internal sex organs have differentiated as female (Figure 18). If the Adam principle then takes over, only the external sex organs are masculinized. This is what happens in the syndrome of female hermaphroditism with congenital adrenal hyperplasia (CAH), which is discussed in Chapter 6.

By contrast, if it is the Adam principle that falters, then the internal sex organs may differentiate as either female or male, depending on when the Eve principle takes over. Under the influence of the Eve principle, the external sex organs are feminized.

When the Adam principle falters, two hormones that may diminish or disappear are androgen and antimullerian hormone. There is no known syndrome in which only androgen, but not antimullerian hormone, disappears. However, there is a condition where antimullerian hormone disappears but androgen remains, and this is known as persistent mullerian duct syndrome.

PERSISTENT MULLERIAN DUCT SYNDROME

Persistent mullerian duct syndrome is a 46,XY chromosomal syndrome in which the embryonic testes of a 46,XY male fail to secrete antimullerian hormone, although they do not fail to secrete androgen. An alternative possibility is that the mullerian ducts are resistant to the hormone that would obliterate them. The outcome is that the mullerian ducts pro-

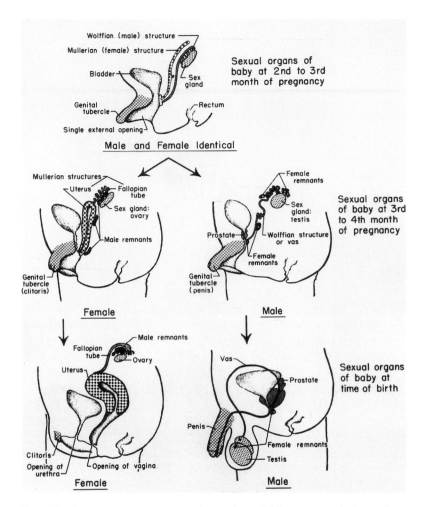

Figure 18. Diagrammatic representation of internal sexual differentiation in the human fetus.

liferate and form a uterus and two fallopian tubes. The baby is born with the testes, scrotum, and penis and with the internal structures of a male, and, in addition, with a female uterus and fallopian tubes (Figure 19). Because of the presence of androgen, which is secreted by the functioning testes, subsequent development in childhood and at puberty is as a male. However, in such individuals, one or both testicles may be confined in the abdominal cavity. When one or the other attempts to descend down the inguinal canal into the scrotum, it may drag some of the female structures with it and become trapped and herniated in the inguinal canal. Investigation of the hernia leads to the diagnosis. The hernia may become evident in infancy, or not until later, after the onset of

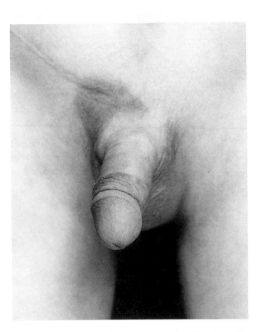

Figure 19. Postoperative picture of a boy in whom the mullerian ducts had developed into a uterus and fallopian tubes. These organs formed a hernia that had been surgically repaired as is evidenced by the scar in the right groin and by the missing left testis.

puberty. It can be corrected surgically. Because surgical intervention is effective, as it is for other types of hernia, long-term postsurgical follow-up is not necessary, and patients become lost to follow-up. They are not routinely referred for counseling. Multiple congenital defects or disabilities are not known to be characteristic of the syndrome. Fertility is possible but cannot be guaranteed. Very few cases have been reported in the medical literature.

Anomalies of the internal reproductive organs are not confined to persistent mullerian duct syndrome. Anomalies of the internal reproductive organs may occur also in combination with anomalies of the external sex organs in male hermaphroditism and true hermaphroditism, as is discussed in the following chapter.

6

External Organ Anomalies: Hermaphroditism

In about the 3rd month of fetal development, the external sexual organs are formed, and Nature continues her bipotential plan, namely, if not Adam, then Eve. At this stage, both males and females begin with the same precursor structures and these precursors are transformed into either female or male external genitalia (Figure 20). It is worthwhile at this point to briefly recapitulate this process. The genital tubercle (Figure 20) grows out to become the penis or retracts to become the clitoris. The skin that wraps around the penis and fuses along the raphe (seam) of the underside to form the foreskin and urethral canal has its counterpart in the hood of the clitoris, which extends lengthwise as the labia minora. The skin of the scrotum, which also fuses and forms a seam along the midline, is the counterpart of the labia majora, which remain unfused to reveal the female genital and urethral openings.

In such a homologous plan of biological engineering, the external genitals may be left unfinished and neither fully masculinized nor fully feminized (Figure 21, see also Figure 11). The unfinished state of either sex looks remarkably like that of the other. From Figure 21, one can see that there is a genital tubercle, which could be either a large clitoris or a small penis. This organ has an open gutter underneath it instead of a covered urethral tube. The urinary orifice is at the root or base of this genital tubercle, more or less in the female position. This urinary orifice may be small and may lead directly to the bladder. Alternatively, underneath the genital tubercle there may be a large urogenital sinus, or funnel-shaped

35

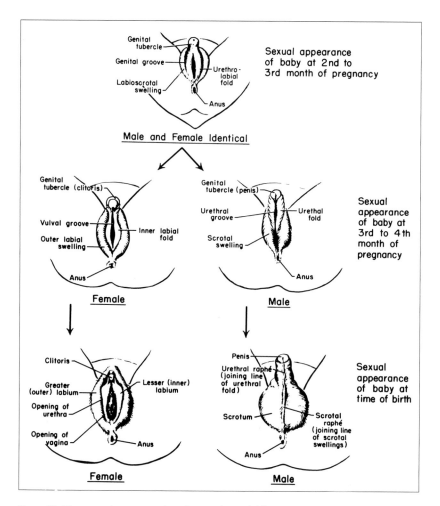

Figure 20. Diagrammatic representation of external sexual differentiation in the human fetus.

cavity, in the interior of which are two orifices, one urethral and the other vaginal. The vaginal passage may either connect with the cervix of the uterus or end blindly. Looked at from the exterior and toward the anus, the urogenital sinus will appear ambiguous and will be similar in form irrespective of whether it represents a scrotum with incomplete fusion or labia majora more fused than they should be.

Incomplete or unfinished external sexual differentiation leaves the physician and parents thoroughly confused as to the sex of a baby. From external appearance alone, such a baby could be identified as a male hermaphrodite, a female hermaphrodite, or a so-called "true" hermaphrodite. According to Klebs's classifactory system (see Chapter 1), a male

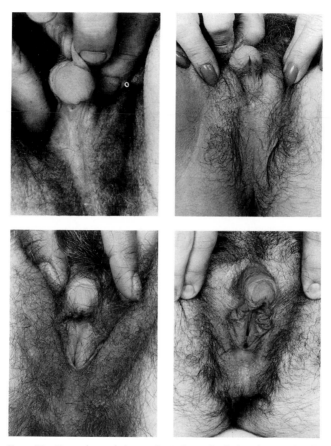

Figure 21. External sexual abnormality in four individuals with 46,XX female hermaphroditism with congenital adrenal hyperplasia (CAH) syndrome, surgically uncorrected, showing four degrees of urogenital closure.

hermaphrodite has two testicles, although sometimes one may be missing, and a female hermaphrodite has two ovaries. (Male and female hermaphroditism are also sometimes called male and female pseudohermaphroditism, respectively.) A true hermaphrodite, by definition, has some ovarian and some testicular tissue either separated or mixed together in the same gonad. All three forms of hermaphroditism are equally genuine or authentic. A synonym for hermaphroditism is intersexuality.

It is not essential to have ambiguous-looking external sex organs to be identified as a hermaphrodite. The ambiguity may exist internally, as in androgen insensitivity syndrome (AIS), already mentioned, or in a male who has a normal penis as well as a uterus. However, the classical dilemma in hermaphroditism is that of the ambiguity of external appearance. For such an individual, it is impossible to tell from external appearance alone whether to classify the condition as female, male, or true hermaphroditism. All three resemble one another, and the names are not the deciding factor in what the sex assignment should be. In medical practice, diagnostic tests enable each form of hermaphroditism to be named according to its etiology, such as AIS or CAH (congenital adrenal hyperplasiaaa; discussed below), unless its etiology remains unknown.

FEMALE HERMAPHRODITISM

Hermaphroditic ambiguity of the sex organs is produced in 46,XX females with two ovaries by an excess of masculinizing hormone (androgen) at the time in prenatal life when the external genitalia are being formed. The most common source of masculinizing hormone is from the fetus itself, for example when malfunctioning adrenocortical glands produce an excess of androgen. This is what results in congenital adrenal hyperplasia (CAH) syndrome, also known as adrenogenital syndrome (Figures 21 and 22). In congenital adrenal hyperplasia, each adrenal cortex does not produce cortisol, as it should, but a closely related androgenic steroid hormone, which is masculinizing. This anomaly is due to a genetic error, carried as a recessive gene known as CYP21B located on the short arm of chromosome 21 and transmitted jointly by both parents on an equal basis. It has been estimated from medical statistics in developed countries that 1:60 males and females carry the recessive gene, but among live births, only 1:7,000 girls actually manifest CAH syndrome (with the same ratio for boys who are not, however, hermaphrodites). In an isolated and inbred community of Yupik Eskimos in Alaska, the incidence of female CAH was 1:141 live births (Pang, Wallace, & Thuline, 1988).

If a couple have one child, male or female, with CAH, then in every subsequent pregnancy there is a one in four probability that CAH will occur again. Prenatal testing is able to show whether the fetus is CAH positive and female. If so, it is possible to begin prenatal hormonal treatment prior to the end of the 2nd month of pregnancy to suppress the appearance of symptoms of masculinization, including genital masculinization in girls. The suppressor is a synthetic adrenocortical hormone, a glucocorticoid, dexamethasone.

Hormonal masculinization in CAH does not cease at birth, but, fortunately, it can be controlled by treatment with regular dosage of the missing adrenocortical hormone, cortisol. The treatment continues throughout life. In times of injury, illness, or stress, the dosage is doubled or tripled if need be in order to imitate the body's normal use of cortisol

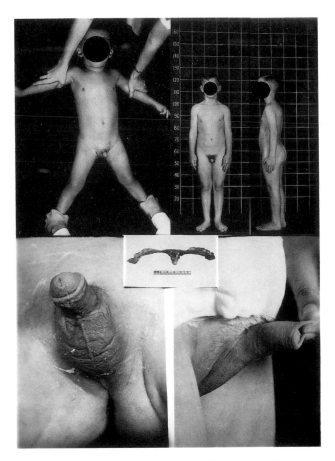

Figure 22. Two cases of complete fetal masculinization in 46,XX congenital adrenal hyperplasia (CAH) syndrome of female hermaphroditism with two ovaries and internal female structures. Both boys continued to live and be medically habilitated as males following diagnosis after early infancy.

as a defense against the stress of injury or disease. If CAH is left untreated, masculinization of growth and development proceeds rapidly. It produces a precociously early male puberty and suppresses the usual signs of female puberty. With treatment, the body feminizes and menstruation occurs (Figure 23).

The configuration of the sex organs at birth renders them subsequently unsuitable for sexual intercourse as either male or female without reconstructive surgery. According to contemporary pediatric policy, the reconstruction is almost always feminizing. Although surgical intervention requires extensive resection of tissue, including reducing a gross-

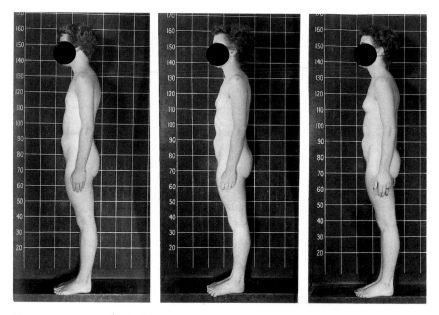

Figure 23. 46,XX congenital adrenal hyperplasia (CAH) syndrome of female hermaphroditism, show-ing the effects of cortisol therapy on breast growth over a period of 18 months. At right, the individual at age 18.

ly enlarged clitoris, erotic sensitivity, although perhaps lessened, is not lost and orgasm is typically possible in later life.

Conception is possible but difficult and may be impossible in the so-called salt-losing variety of CAH. Delivery by cesarean section is virtually inevitable as the birth canal is likely to be too narrow for vaginal delivery.

Erotic attraction to males may be weak to absent, and may be replaced by attraction to females in perhaps 10% of individuals, if not more. Being erotically attracted to females is more acceptable in those few instances in which the individual has been declared and reared as a boy, with all hormonal and surgical management geared toward mas-culinization.

Intellectual development in CAH is skewed toward the upper end of the IQ distribution. High academic and career achievement are well rep-resented. It is possible that the genetic factor responsible for CAH is linked to another genetic factor responsible for intellectual superiority.

The counseling program for individuals with CAH and their families follows the principles that are outlined further in Chapter 13. As in all disorders that require lifetime maintenance or medication, compliancy is a prevalent counseling topic. Remembering the need for an increased dosage of cortisol when under the stress of injury or illness is essential. The individuals with CAH and their families must become confidently assertive on this issue in cases of emergency as, for example, when away from home. Wearing a registered medical alert bracelet is an excellent expedient. In adolescence, when girls with CAH need personalized sexological counseling, many of them become resistant and noncompliant. As they get older, self-disclosure becomes easier.

In some very rare individuals with female hermaphroditism, the excess of masculinizing hormone may be due to an androgen-secreting tumor that developed in the mother during the pregnancy. Another possibility, once more common but no longer, is that the mother might have taken a hormonal preparation that had an adverse side effect on the fetus. In the 1940s and 1950s, newly discovered synthetic sex hormones, for example diethylstilbestrol (DES), were widely prescribed in the belief, later proved false, that they would prevent pregnancy loss. Genital malformation was one of the side effects. A similar type of genital malformation was caused during the same years by progestinic steroidal hormones. Progestinic steroidal hormones were administered as pregnancy-saving hormones, and the condition they produced became known as progestin-induced hermaphroditism (Figure 24).

MALE HERMAPHRODITISM

Male hermaphroditism refers to a birth defect of the sex organs with no ovarian tissue present, only testicular tissue. The testicular tissue may be present on one side only or on both sides and may be completely formed or incompletely formed. In effect, male hermaphroditism is a mixed bag

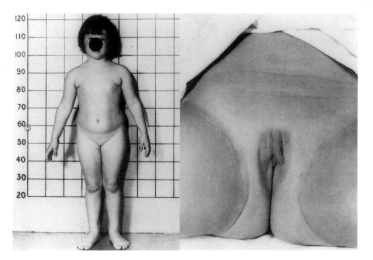

Figure 24.   Progestin-induced hermaphroditism in a female showing clitoral enlargement.

of what is left over after female hermaphroditism (ovarian tissue only) and true hermaphroditism (both ovarian and testicular tissue) have been ruled out. The mixed bag of male hermaphroditism contains syndromes as unlike one another as androgen insensitivity syndrome, persistent mullerian duct syndrome (partial or complete), and the syndromes of partial testicular masculinization about to be considered. What they share in common is the presence of testicular tissue and, in most cases, a 46,XY chromosome count, although XY mosaicism, as in 45,X/46,XY, is also included.

In a fetus with a 46,XY chromosome count, partial or incomplete testicular masculinization may be the outcome of a partial inability of the fetal testicular tissue to produce either the amount or the type of hormone needed to masculinize the sexual anatomy. An alternative possibility is that incomplete testicular masculinization may be due to a defect in the cells of the target tissues which, in turn, prevents them from absorbing enough of the hormone needed for masculinization.

There is also a variety of male hermaphroditism in which the internal masculine organs are more complete on one side of the body than on the other. On the incomplete side, there is only a gonadal streak. Testicular tissue is on the other side only. In addition, on the side of the streak, the internal masculine reproductive structures (see Figure 18) may be absent and replaced by malformed feminine structures that developed from the mullerian ducts. These feminine structures typically take the form of a single fallopian tube and a malformed uterus. Their presence may be suspected by palpation during a physical examination. For confirmation, a noninvasive ultrasound sonogram may suffice, whereas it once was necessary to resort to exploratory surgery.

For the newborn, there is a method to determine if incomplete masculinization is attributable to the failure of testicular tissue or of target tissue. The method is to apply an ointment containing male sex hormone, testosterone propionate, to the genital area for 6 weeks or more. If the sex organs do not respond by showing color and size changes similar to those that occur at puberty, this indicates that the sex organs are androgen-insensitive and will not respond normally at puberty. This is a sign also that masculinization at puberty will not take place and will be replaced by feminization, which cannot be reversed and replaced by masculinization. The breasts will grow, the voice will remain high pitched, and there will be sparse or no growth of facial or body hair (Figure 25).

For an individual with this anomaly who lives as a male, the penis is too short for sexual intercourse, and its erectile response is inadequate. The fluid of ejaculation is minimal or absent. Pleasant erotic feeling is not missing, but it does not reach the full climactic peak of orgasm. The great-

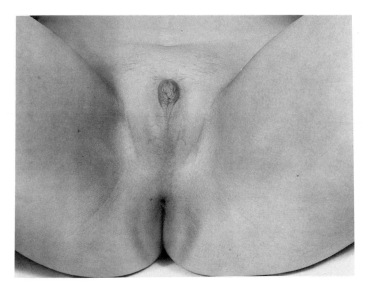

Figure 25. Incomplete masculinization in a 46,XY male hermaphrodite, who should have been declared and reared as a girl instead of as a boy. He elected at age 15 to be surgically and hormonally reassigned as a female.

est difficulty for the individual is not erotic and sexual, but the failure to achieve the typical appearance of an adult and of always being mistaken as younger than the chronological age. The disparity is so great that one individual at age 32 was always responded to by strangers as if he were 16 or 17 and in the company of his wife was addressed as her son. His body was unresponsive to male hormone treatments (Figure 26).

By contrast, the individual who does respond to male hormone treatment is the one for whom incomplete masculinization is attributable to a deficiency or failure of testicular hormone secretion. For this individual, the testosterone propionate ointment test in infancy will produce color and size changes in the sex organs. If the application of ointment is continued for several months, the hypospadiac, malformed penis may enlarge so that it appears almost normal in size for a boy, which allows it to be more effectively repaired surgically. However, it will not enlarge for a second time when the rest of the body matures into adulthood.

If the deficiency or failure of testicular hormone function persists at puberty, then male hormone replacement therapy should be given to induce and, if necessary, maintain adult masculine maturation. However, pubertal maturation may begin of its own accord.

One type of 46,XY male hermaphroditism in which masculinizing puberty begins of its own accord is brought about by a deficiency in prenatal life of the enzyme 5α-reductase. Without enough of this enzyme to

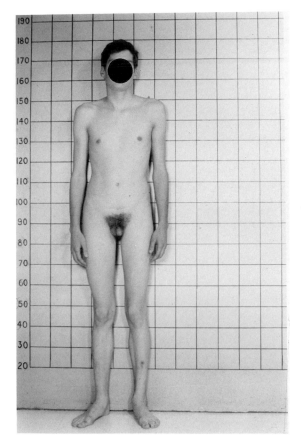

Figure 26.   Androgen insensitivity syndrome (AIS) in a 46,XY male hermaphrodite with a very small, surgically repaired hypospadiac phallus. Breasts have been surgically removed, as have the feminizing testes. At age 23, there is an absence of aging as well as evidence of incomplete virilization. Erection was not possible. Scrotum contains artificial testes.

convert testosterone into dihydrotestosterone within the precursor cells of the genitalia, the Adam principle fails, the Eve principle takes over, and the external sexual anatomy at birth resembles that of a female. Later in life, at the age of puberty, there is a surprising and unexplained reversal toward masculinization that especially affects the voice, muscular growth, and the enlargement of what in childhood had appeared to be a clitoris.

There are no statistics concerning the incidence of the 46,XY 5α-reductase deficiency syndrome in the population at large. As mentioned in Chapter 1, a concentration of several generations of individuals with this syndrome has been discovered in two isolated and inbred communities. Contemporary medical policy is not unanimous regarding sex of assignment and rearing. For individuals to live successfully as girls, it is necessary that they be assigned as girls at birth and that surgical, hormonal, and social management be feminizing from infancy onward.

It is a general rule that the greater the degree of failure of the Adam principle, the greater is the likelihood that a newborn baby with a diagnosis of male hermaphroditism should be declared a girl and reared as a girl, with surgical and hormonal case management directed toward feminization (see Figure 25). The surgical attempt at masculine reconstruction of a missing or minuscule penis has a less than satisfactory outcome. The penis is the only organ in the body that contains the spongy tissue (corpora cavernosa) responsible for erection. Thus there is no possibility of enlarging a small penis with a graft of spongy tissue transplanted from elsewhere in the body. There is no particular corresponding obstacle to feminizing reconstructive surgery.

If the life experiences of a 46,XY male hermaphrodite reared as a girl lead the individual to conclude that a change of sex is essential, the very name of the condition, male hermaphroditism, predisposes professionals to support that conclusion and to provide hormonal and surgical sex reassignment as a male. By contrast, it is difficult for an individual with the same type of male hermaphroditism to get professional approval for male-to-female sex reassignment so as to live as a woman, even if the alternative is suicide. Psychological, religious, or any other form of therapeutic counseling against sex reassignment is ineffectual. Therefore, the possibility of male-to-female reassignment should never be categorically excluded. Professional refusal in some instances may be inhumane and may, in effect, constitute malpractice.

TRUE HERMAPHRODITISM

The combination of ovarian and testicular tissue, which is the criterion for true hermaphroditism, may be present as a mixed ovotestis on both sides, or on one side only with an ovary or a testis on the other. In rare individuals, there is no ovotestis but an ovary on one side and a testicle on the other, which may or may not be descended (Figure 27).

In ancient Greek and Roman statues, Hermaphroditus was depicted as a boy with breasts (see Figure 1). There is a popular misconception that a true hermaphrodite has the complete sexual anatomy of both a male and a female and is capable of self-fertilization. Embryologically, this myth of the hermaphrodite as a sort of Siamese twin capable of producing ova and sperms and of having the internal organs prerequisite to pregnancy is untenable. Usually, either the Adam or the Eve principle

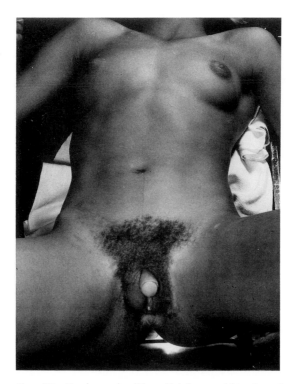

Figure 27.   True hermaphroditism with left ovary, right testis, and 46,XX chromosome count. Individual was surgically and hormonally treated as a male. He lived as a male, married, and became a stepfather.

predominates internally, although each may be imperfectly represented, one on each side of the body, as in Figure 27.

True hermaphroditism once was considered a sufficient medical rarity that each newly ascertained case was reported in the medical literature. The novelty wore off after the total reached around 300 in the 1960s–1970s. The actual incidence of true hermaphroditism is not known. The chromosome count may be 46,XY or 46,XX/46,XY, but the chromosome count is predominantly 46,XX. It is presumed that male-determining genetic material from the Sex-determining Region (SRY) of a Y chromosome has spliced itself into one of the X chromosomes or another one of the 46 chromosomes. The same presumption is made in the case of the rare occurrence of 46,XX males who are not hermaphrodites genitally.

Hermaphroditism that would be diagnosed as "true" may pass undetected unless there is a diagnostic work-up that includes a sonogram and possible exploratory surgery (Figure 28) to ascertain the structure of the gonads. If the diagnosis is made neonatally, the declared sex should be

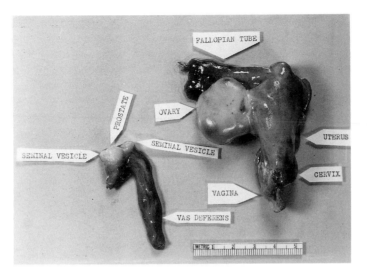

Figure 28.   The internal organs of both sexes found surgically in the case of true hermaphroditism shown in Figure 27. The single testicle remained in place in the right scrotum.

influenced by the prospects of fertility as male or female, and by the post-surgical prospects of successful sexual intercourse as a male or female. If the diagnosis of true hermaphroditism is not established until later in life, then the individual should continue to live as a member of the sex to which his or her gender-identity/role (G-I/R) already belongs, with congruent surgical and hormonal intervention, as needed.

7

External Organ Anomalies: Non-hermaphroditic

The five anomalies presented in this chapter share three characteristics: 1) they are not diagnosable as one of the varieties of hermaphroditism although the methods of intervention may be similar; 2) they are congenital and probably genetic in origin, although their precise etiology remains unidentified; and 3) they all affect the reproductive anatomy.

HYPOSPADIAS

Hypospadias is an abnormality of the penis in which the meatus (urinary opening) opens on the underside of the penis. In its most extreme form, it occurs in hermaphroditism. The penis has an unfused open gutter instead of a closed urethral tube on its underside, and the urinary orifice is at the base instead of the tip (Figure 29). At the other end of the scale is a mild form of hypospadias in which the urinary orifice is only 1 or 2 mm displaced from its proper position. Mild hypospadias does not hinder effective urination or copulation and so does not need surgical intervention as do the more severe forms. Other things being equal, it is desirable for a boy to begin school with a severe hypospadias corrected. For the best surgical result, however, it may not be advisable to complete the surgical repair so early before the penis has a good size. In this circumstance, sexual counseling is imperative so that the boy understands his condition and the predictability of surgical reconstruction. He needs also to be provided with options for privacy in urination—for example, learning the

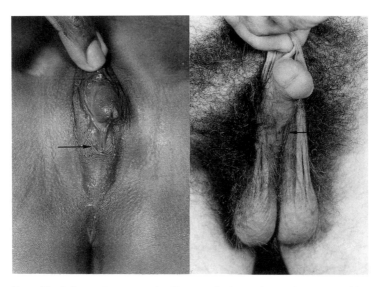

Figure 29. Left, an extreme example of hypospadias in a male, creating an external her-maphroditic appearance. The testes are undescended. Right, a lesser example of hypospa-dias. The arrows point to the urinary openings. On the right, the father; on the left, his son.

location of the toilets before the first day of school and having permission to use them unaccompanied. Later, he may want to be exempted from undressing in the school shower or locker room.

At all ages, all children need to know in advance what is planned surgically when they go to the operating room. In this case, mystified by the unknown, a boy can easily conjecture that he will emerge from the operation minus the penis that he treasures and hopes will one day be a good one. When admitted for hypospadiac repair, an older boy needs an explanation of his hospitalization to give to his school friends and acquaintances. He is best advised to give a simple statement about a "uri-nary blockage" or "problem of infection."

Hypospadias may or may not be accompanied by undescended testes. If undescended, they may come down of their own accord or under the influence of hormonal treatment that imitates the beginning of puberty. In some individuals, the testes will remain undescended or missing. If missing, prosthetic testes made of silicone and soft to the touch can be put in place. Prosthetic testes may be essential to a boy or man for the sake of appearance and personal sexological well-being.

Artificial hypospadias, with the opening of the urethra displaced a short distance down the shaft from the tip of the penis, may be the out-come of a badly performed circumcision. There are also individuals whose entire penis has been burned off by the faulty use of a surgical cauterizer in circumcision.

Circumcision of newborn males was not much practiced in America until after 1870, at which time it was popularized, falsely, as a cure for masturbation in adolescence. Today, although other rationales are argued in its defense, circumcision is justifiably under attack as a costly, unnecessary, and extremely painful form of surgery, and some medical insurance plans do not pay for it.

The origin of the custom of circumcision is lost in prehistory, as is also the custom of the Australian aboriginals of subincising the urethra, slitting it open from the tip of the penis to the base, to create an artificial hypospadias with the urinary opening in a feminine position. Both customs could have their origins in blood sacrifice and could be attenuated forms of human sacrifice and symbolic substitutes for it. In some societies, notably in East Africa and South Arabia, the hood of the clitoris and the labia minora and labia majora are removed in mutilatory ritual circumcision of females at age 6 or 7 (Lightfoot-Klein, 1989). The procedure is gruesomely painful and medically dangerous. Ritual circumcision of males has wide ethnographic range and is known from Australia to the Middle East. It is an obligatory religious ritual for Jews and Moslems. In non-Jewish America and elsewhere, especially where babies are born in hospitals, it is done ostensibly for hygienic reasons, but far more likely is simply an example of what, in anthropological terminology, is cultural borrowing.

EPISPADIAS

In some individuals, a birth defect of the sex organs is part of a larger malformation that involves also the urinary and/or defecatory system. Epispadias (Figure 30) is a severe condition in which the bladder empties directly through a gaping orifice in the lower abdominal wall, with the penis itself in a male, or the clitoris in a female, appearing to be split in half along the center line of its dorsal (upward) side. Surgical repair is possible for both males and females, but urinary continence may be a problem in both sexes. In the male, the repaired penis may be too small for adequate coitus, may not be quite correctly situated, and may not be capable of full erection. In males who have the most severe cases and who have a very small, very deformed penis, it may be advisable at birth to declare the child a female, and to undertake feminizing surgical repair, as is done in penile agenesis and extreme micropenis (discussed below). If the penis is big enough to function coitally in adulthood, the more usual procedure is to repair the male with epispadias as a male.

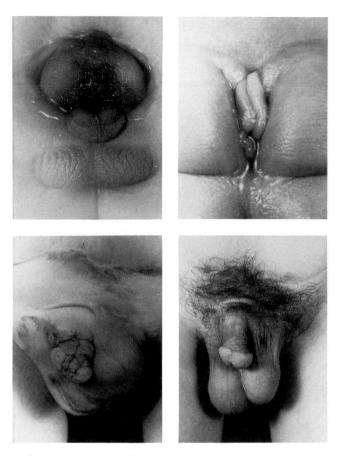

Figure 30. Epispadias at birth, with congenital malformation (exstrophy) of the bladder in a male (top left) and a female (top right). Below are two stages of surgical repair in the same male, at ages 7 and 14.

PHIMOSIS

Circumcision may be performed as an intervention for phimosis, a congenital condition in which the foreskin, if forced back, is so tight that it painfully constricts the neck of the penis, as if the foreskin were a tight rubber band, as depicted in Figure 31 before and after retraction of the foreskin. Alternatively, tightness may be surgically loosened by repositioning tissue without removing it. There is also the possibility of gently retracting and stretching the foreskin in progressive self-dilating exercise. If regular sexual activity is established, either masturbation or sexual intercourse may stretch and loosen the foreskin satisfactorily.

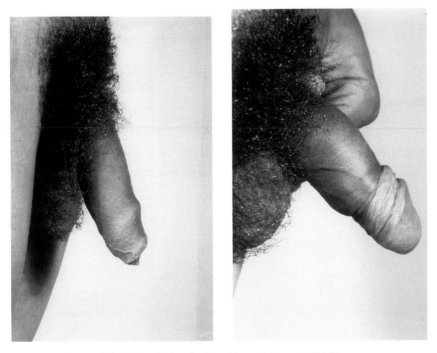

Figure 31.   Phimosis (left) evidenced when the skin of the penis is retracted (right).

MICROPENIS

Penile agenesis is a birth defect in which the penis is totally missing and the urethral opening is located on the rim of the anus. Micropenis is a birth defect in which the penis is in its correct position but extremely short, typically between 1 and 2 cm, and is, for the most part, a skinny tube with a vestigial internal spongy structure and a small glans at the tip (Figure 32). The testes are usually small and defective in this anomaly, and the internal genitalia may be defective also and possibly hermaphroditic. Micropenis may be associated with one of various genetic syndromes, or it may occur in isolation. There are no statistics as to the prevalence of micropenis and no explanation of its cause other than as a developmental, genetic error.

It is true that penises come in all sizes, as do hands and feet, and may bear very little relationship to the size of the body. Although size may be a matter of male vanity, a great deal of variance is allowable before a penis is too big to permit satisfactory coitus or too small to do so. Generalized obesity is likely to be a coital handicap if the penis is also small, by hiding the retracted penis under a roll of fat. In a genuine case

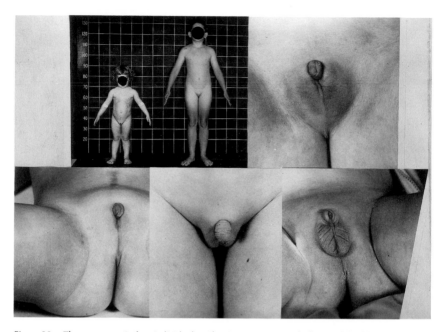

Figure 32.   The sex organs in four individuals with micropenis (microphallus) and the full view of two of them; one surgically corrected to be reared as a girl (left), the other reared as a boy (right).

of extreme micropenis, however, the organ is definitely too small to permit satisfactory copulation in adulthood. It is, therefore, fairly common to recommend to the parents that they raise a male baby with micropenis as a girl. This is, of course, a very difficult decision for parents to make, and they must be given all the information possible to understand the rationale and consequences of the decision. First and foremost, they need to know that gender identity and role are not preordained by genetic and intrauterine events alone, but that their differentiation is also very much a postnatal process and highly responsive to social stimulation and experience. Thus, they may need to be reassured that their baby can grow up socially as a girl and fall in love as a female. Surgical correction of the newborn will give the child the visible appearance of a girl, and a second-stage surgical intervention in teenage or young adulthood when the body is full-grown can construct a vagina adequate for intercourse. The outcome of vaginoplasty too early in childhood is unsatisfactory. Hormonal replacement treatment in the early teens can ensure the physique and appearance of a female. Fertility is not seriously an issue, since it is unlikely that the testes would have been fertile if they had been left in place. In some individuals, they may have been feminizing testes, and in other individuals, prone to cancer.

In individuals with micropenis, if there is to be a reannouncement of the baby's sex, it is of crucial importance that the parents have the conviction that they will be able to complete what they begin. Only then will they be able to rear the child consistently as a girl. If they are in doubt, then their ambivalence will almost certainly communicate itself to the child. To some degree, the conviction will express itself in their equanimity in answering whatever questions their child may ask and in breaking the ice to offer information that the child certainly will need. Their most effective strategy may be to refer emotion-laden issues to the child's doctor or a sexological counselor. They themselves can rely very much on the explanatory formula of the child's having been born sexually unfinished.

Boys who have a penis that, although larger than a micropenis, is extremely small, will benefit from counseling. Such a boy is particularly in need of a knowledgeable outsider to whom he can reveal, in confidence, such secret thoughts as perhaps he should be a girl. The conjectures and ruminations of childhood go much deeper and are more vital to a child than adults sometimes care to face.

It has proved possible for some individuals with a miniature penis to ameliorate some of the distress of childhood by the application of testosterone ointment locally to the penis, as has been mentioned in connection with 46,XY hermaphroditism. The male sex hormone in the ointment produces what is actually a localized puberty. The penis grows, sparse pubic hair appears, and the boost in morale is great. The positive effects overshadow the fact that the treatment only accelerates the growth of the penis to its adult size and that it will not become much larger when testosterone may need to be given again later, orally or by injection, so that the rest of the body enters puberty. However, the increase in morale may enable a boy to join in sports and gym, and to appear naked before age-mates.

As he approaches his teens, he can learn in more detail about his prospects for sexual intercourse and about techniques of erotic stimulation and about the use of an artificial or prosthetic penis for the stimulation of his partner in coitus. By knowing in advance about future possibilities, a boy with micropenis will be better prepared to go through the adolescent phases of social and romantic development. Eventually he should be able to find someone whose erotic search reciprocates his own, provided he does not lose hope.

VAGINAL ATRESIA

Vaginal atresia is an anomaly in which there is a shallow vaginal pouch of insufficient depth for coitus, or only a dimple to represent the vaginal orifice. This condition is found in two syndromes. The first is the 46,XY androgen insensitivity syndrome (AIS) already discussed in Chapter 4. The second syndrome is its counterpart, Meyer-Rokitansky-Küster syndrome (MRKS), which occurs in 46,XX women with two ovaries (Figure 33).

MRKS is a congenital condition, the outcome of an error of embryological development of unknown cause. It has been known to occur more than once in a family pedigree, but usually not. It affects only the mullerian organs (uterus and fallopian tubes), which may be either unformed, or imperfectly formed. The ovaries are normally in place. The symptom that first brings it to attention is failure of the onset of menstrual periods. The gynecologist then discovers that in the place of the vagina there is either a dimple or a shallow pouch that does not connect with the cervix. In most individuals, the uterus is represented by a cord-like structure with no cavity from which to produce menstrual bleeding. In exceptional cases a uterine cavity is well enough formed to produce menstrual blood that becomes trapped and painful as there is no vaginal orifice from which to menstruate. That condition can be corrected surgically, as well as can the shallowness of a blind vagina.

Instead of undergoing surgical vaginoplasty, if the vagina is not a dimple but a shallow cavity, a woman with MRKS syndrome may, like some AIS women (see Chapter 4), elect to lengthen the vagina by self-dilation. If surgical vaginoplasty is the only alternative, then the individual with MRKS, whether a teenager or older, should be allowed to elect

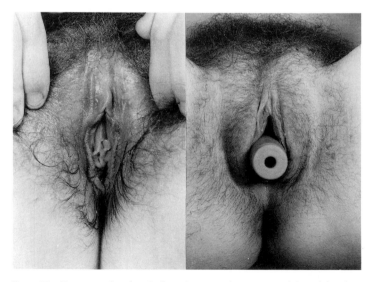

Figure 33.   Two examples of vaginal atresia; external appearance (left) and the placement of a form after surgery to lengthen a too-short vaginal canal (right).

the timing of surgery so that it fits with other agenda in her life's schedule. In times past, it used to be prudishly recommended to delay surgery until marriage, but such thinking no longer prevails.

It is important for girls—and boys, too—with any type of birth defect of the sex organs to rehearse ahead of time what they will say about themselves to the different people who push them for an explanation. It is equally important that the individual and his or her parents agree on a formula so that they do not tell inconsistent stories. Their primary health care providers should be able to give valuable suggestions and terminology.

8

Hypothalamic Anomalies and Sexual Orientation

The hypothalamus is a pea-sized region of the brain that is situated in the middle of the head behind the bridge of the nose. The hypothalamus communicates with the rest of the brain on a wide-ranging information highway, and is densely interconnected within its own borders (Figures 34 and 35). Despite its small size, the hypothalamus has an amazingly diverse and prolific influence on the essential vital processes of survival and reproduction. It is connected to and governs its satellite organ, the pituitary gland. Through neurochemical messengers, the hypothalamus instructs the pituitary gland to secrete gonadotropins (from the Greek *gonad,* ovary or testis, and *tropos,* turning or approaching). Gonadotropins travel in the bloodstream and in turn instruct the ovaries and testes to make their female and male hormones, respectively.

In prenatal life, with a possible extension into early neonatal life, clusters of cells in the posterior part of the hypothalamus develop under the influence of the same sex hormones that form the sex organs. If the Eve principle prevails, these hypothalamic cell clusters, or nuclei, regulate the hormonal cycles of the pituitary gland so that in subprimate mammals periods of heat (estrus) occur and in primates, periods of menstruation occur, with or without estrus. If the Adam principle prevails, then there are no equivalent hormonal cycles.

Situated very close to these posterior hypothalamic nuclei are cell clusters of the anterior hypothalamus. Some of the cell clusters of the anterior hypothalamus are responsible for the regulation of mating behavior in synchrony with the hormonal cycles of the female in species that go into heat (estrus). In the lower animal species, the female's cycle

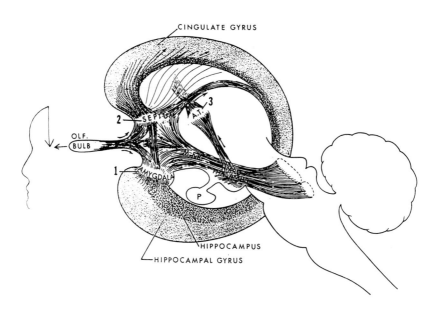

Figure 34. Schematic diagram showing location of hypothalamus and its connection in the human brain.

influences the male, for example, by way of vaginal odors (pheromones) for which the male's nose is very sensitive, or by way of genital coloration that reaches the male's brain through the eyes. In laboratory animal studies, a male/female difference has been found in the overall magnitude of some of the nuclei of the anterior hypothalamus, or in the size of the cells they contain. Hence, they are termed sexually dimorphic. Sexually dimorphic nuclei are found in the human hypothalamus as well as in that of other animal species.

It is not known whether in human males and females there are anterior hypothalamic nuclei that regulate the incidence of sexual behavior or the occurrence of sexual imagery and thoughts. Experiments with male monkeys, however, suggest that such centers may exist, at least in males. These monkeys were given an injection of radioactive anti-male hormone that could be traced in the body. As soon as 15 minutes after the injection, the hormone could be located in anterior hypothalamic cells (Rees, Bonsall, & Michael, 1986). In addition, the hormone induced a decline in sexual behavior even when the level of testosterone in the bloodstream was kept artificially high (Michael & Zumpe, 1993).

It is ethically forbidden to do a corresponding experiment on human males, but, toward the end of the 1980s, it became possible to search for homosexual/heterosexual differences in the nuclei of the anterior hypothalamus because some homosexual men dying of human immuno-

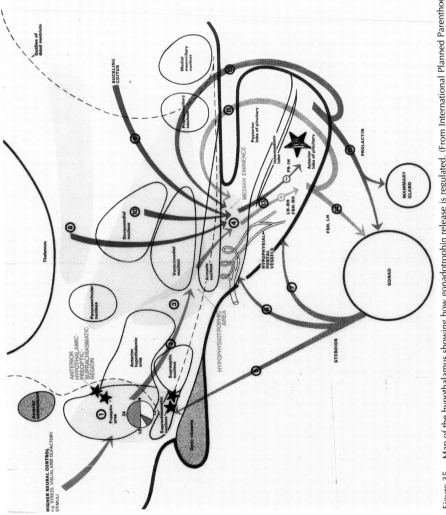

Figure 35. Map of the hypothalamus showing how gonadotrophin release is regulated. (From International Planned Parenthood Federation; reprinted by permission.)

deficiency virus/acquired immunodeficiency syndrome (HIV/AIDS) bequeathed their brains to medical research. Three different investigators each found a nucleus or location of the male hypothalamus that showed a homosexual/heterosexual difference in either cell count, cell size, or both (Allen & Gorski, 1992; LeVay, 1991; Swaab & Hofman, 1990). As always in science, these findings need to be replicated before they can be accepted with confidence. If these differences are sufficiently replicated and confirmed also in females, it will be necessary to find out what function each of the three different hypothalamic locations serves and what aspect of sexual orientation, if any, each influences. Furthermore, it will be necessary to ascertain at what age, prenatally or postnatally, the homosexual/heterosexual difference first appeared, how it was engineered, and whether it is immutably fixed or changeable. Irrespective of its location in the brain, and of how or when it got there, a totally homosexual or a totally heterosexual orientation, with no bisexual possibility, is for many people as immutable as left-handedness or color-blindness. An immutable sexual orientation is something that the individual and society simply must adapt to and live with.

It is scientifically too early to attempt to link homosexual and heterosexual differences in the hypothalamus to the genetic code. However, in gene mapping, the search is underway for the genetics of sexual orientation as homosexual or heterosexual. Hamer, Hu, Magnuson, Hu, and Pattatucci (1993) reported a study of 114 kinships in each of which there was a self-identified homosexual male. They found an increased rate of male homosexuality in the maternal but not the paternal side of the family, namely in maternal uncles and in cousins who were sons of maternal aunts. That led, in a study of 40 pairs of homosexual brothers and their kinfolk, to the finding of a relationship of homosexuality to DNA markers on the X chromosome (inherited from the mother) at position Xq28. These markers were found in 64% of the homosexual brothers. The full significance of this finding, if confirmed, for genetics and the origin of sexual orientation cannot as yet even be conjectured. Genetics may represent only the first of a cascading series of events all of which must occur, either prenatally or postnatally, or both, if homosexuality is to eventuate.

Step by step in the course of prenatal life, male and female differentiation of the body is preceded by a state of bipotentiality that either resolves into monopotentiality (male or female) or remains a state of partially unresolved bipotentiality. Otherwise stated, there is an Adam/Eve state that becomes either Adam or Eve, or else remains in-between. For example, the external genital anatomy, initially bipotential, becomes that of either Adam or Eve, with the in-between, Adam/Eve exception of hermaphroditic ambiguity.

Hypothetically, the same principle applies to male and female sexuo-erotic differentiation within the brain and mind. The initial bipotential state is conventionally referred to as ambisexual or bisexual. When bisexuality resolves into monosexuality, monosexuality is expressed as either feminine or masculine. Monosexual feminine and masculine sexuoerotic differentiation begin prenatally and continue postnatally. Feminine and masculine sexuoerotic identities may differentiate in either concordance or discordance with the external genitals as female or male, respectively. As applied to sexuoerotic orientation, monosexual femininity in a woman is heterosexually oriented, whereas in a man, monosexual femininity is homosexually oriented. Correspondingly, monosexual masculinity in a man is heterosexually oriented, whereas in a woman it is homosexually oriented.

In bisexuality, the bipotential pendulum gets permanently set, sexuoerotically, at neither a homosexual nor heterosexual position, exclusively. In a bisexual orientation, homosexuality as well as heterosexuality is coded in the brain. In other words, the brain encodes two gendermaps, one for homosexuality and one for heterosexuality, and in bisexuals both are working maps. (A gendermap is a template, schema, or pattern in the brain and mind.)

In the fixated homosexual, the heterosexual gendermap is latent; in the fixated heterosexual, the homosexual gendermap is latent. Latent does not mean nonexistent, however. A latent map codes information and directions that specify where not to go or be. A latent map may stay that way in perpetuity, but there is no guarantee that it will. There are, in fact, some individuals in whom a predominantly heterosexual orientation changes spontaneously to a predominantly homosexual one. Similarly, a predominantly homosexual orientation in an individual may also change to a predominantly heterosexual one. When such a change takes place, it must be assumed that the change also takes place in the brain, although it can be diagnosed in the brain only in rare cases, for example, when brain surgery is needed for a brain tumor in a person who has undergone a change of orientation at the same time as developing the brain tumor.

The discovery of a homosexual/heterosexual difference in the brain in and of itself tells nothing about the source of that difference, or when it first appeared. The difference might have antecedents in the hormonal coding of the brain in prenatal life, which itself may or may not have been genetically coded. Instead of ceasing at birth, hormonal coding of the brain may well extend into the first several weeks of life, insofar as there is a major difference between males and females in the blood levels of sex hormones at that time (Migeon & Forest, 1983). In girls, the prenatal level of all sex hormones rapidly declines to near zero where it stays until the pubertal increase begins. In boys, by contrast, after a 2-week period of decline, there is a rapid climb in the level of testosterone, the male sex hormone, until it reaches the same magnitude as is found at puberty. Then the flood tide recedes until it is near zero at about the age of 3 months, where it remains until puberty begins. What effect, if any, this testosterone surge has on the hypothalamus or any other part of the brain has not yet been ascertained. In addition, nothing has yet been ascertained regarding other brain chemistries that may shape the development of human erotic orientation.

It is known from laboratory studies of neonatal rats, however, that the level of the neurotransmitter serotonin in the brain's hypothalamic region is higher in females than in males in the newborn period and that this difference correlates with behavioral feminization and demasculinization of mating and other responses in adulthood (Wilson, Gonzales, & Farabollini, 1991; Wilson, Pearson, Hunter, Tuohy, & Payne, 1986).

One of the great mysteries awaiting future brain research is how practice effects, imprinting, learning, and remembering become coded in the chemistries of the brain so as to have a permanent neurochemical effect on brain functioning, including hypothalamic functioning, and possibly on submicroscopic brain structure as well. Enough research has been done to demonstrate conclusively that learning and remembering, especially at critical periods of development, do have a permanent effect on the neuroanatomy and function of the brain and on the behavioral and mental functions it governs. Thus, it is quite feasible to work on the assumption that hypothalamic neuroanatomical differences between heterosexual and homosexual brains are, at least in part, a manifestation of the developmental biology of learning and remembering. Learning and remembering need not be here today and gone tomorrow. Sometimes they are permanent, as in the case of imprinting.

The hypothalamus has also another sexual role not specifically related to sex differences, but connected with timing of puberty. It is quite likely that within the hypothalamus a biological clock exists that regulates the timing of puberty, perhaps in cooperation with the biological clock of the two suprachiasmic nuclei (major nerve centers in the hypothalamus) and with as yet unidentified connections in the nearby limbic system and the temporal lobe of the cerebral cortex.

9

Anomalies of Assignment and Rearing

The assignment of sex to a newborn is the product of a public announcement, an official act through the signing of the birth certificate, and a reiterative routine in all the daily acts of rearing that defines and stereotypes masculine and feminine roles and expectancies. The rearing of an anatomically normal child contrary to the natal assignment of sex is almost unknown. When it does occur, one or both parents or caregivers can be presumed to be psychotic. However, it is a different matter when parents become caught up in the drama of assigning sex to a child born with abnormal sex organs.

The drama may begin when prenatal genetic testing reveals a chromosome abnormality or when a prenatal sonogram indicates a probable defect of the genitalia. It is more likely, however, to begin in the delivery room where, not uncommonly, none of those present has rehearsed what to say or do when a child is born with any kind of defect. In the case of a birth defect of the sex organs, it is unwise to pronounce the baby a boy or a girl, he or she, on the basis of a cursory inspection of the external organs, particularly if the mother is awake and the father is present at the delivery. Those nouns and pronouns convey certainty. They foster the conviction that the baby is *really* a boy or a girl, no matter what else may be explained later, should the original pronouncement be rescinded. It is preferable to say at the outset that the baby's sex is indeterminant, and it is advisable to delay the public announcement of sex until a definite decision has been reached, pending further investigation. To delay a public announcement is relatively straightforward, whereas to delay use of the pronouns he and she is virtually impossible. It is too difficult to keep referring to a newborn baby as it, as might have been done, jokingly, before birth. Most people fall into the habit of using he or she, although knowing it to be provisional. The longer the usage continues, the harder it is to relinquish. Thus, it is highly desirable not to prolong the procedures that are needed in order to reach finality and consensus on the baby's assigned sex.

Reaching consensus is not always as straightforward or as speedy as it might be. Different people, professionals included, have different criteria for resolving the issue of sex assignment. There are some who swear by genetics and await the report from the genetics laboratory. Others swear by the ancient wisdom of fertility and await the definitive report on the status of the ovaries or testicles.

For the average person, it is simply a matter of common sense that ovaries and testicles, if not the genetics of chromosomes, are the ultimate biological markers of whether a baby is male or female. The very idea of a biological marker, however, assumes unity among all markers, so that one predicts all of the others. However, this is not so in the case of birth defects of the sex organs. Therefore, neither chromosomes nor ovarian or testicular tissue can be the ultimate criterion of what the sex of assignment should be. Predictions based on them may be wrong. This is why it is necessary to consider what will happen with the hormonalization of puberty and how well the genitalia can be surgically reconstructed to function in the male or female copulatory role in adulthood. "Too small now, too small later" is a useful working rule with regard to surgical construction or reconstruction of a penis. Thus, if use of a pronoun cannot be postponed, use the pronoun she rather than he while awaiting the final verdict on the declaration of the sex of a baby whose external genitals look definitely not masculine. If a change must be made, then it should be made only once and forever, with no delay or vacillation.

Very few parents-to-be have ever had the idea of a birth defect of the sex organs so much as cross their minds. There are no fundraising campaigns that bring such conditions to public attention, and no support groups for affected families and their children. To admit to having a birth defect of the sex organs in the family is for many people, unfortunately, the equivalent of a social disgrace. A few families turn to a religious leader as the ultimate arbiter of God's will regarding the baby's sex, but the majority turn to medical experts.

When a reannouncement of sex is necessary, the advice given to parents may be to move to a new town, find a new job, sever all connections with the past, and start life anew. For most families, that formula is completely untenable. People who have followed it live haunted lives, pursued by ghosts of their past and constantly intimidated by them. There is always the nagging and realistic fear that somehow their secret will come out, for it is impossible to guarantee total obliteration of one's past.

The recommended alternative is to deal with the reannouncement openly. As the first step, the parents need to have the necessary medical information, albeit somewhat simplified, in order to be able to explain their dilemma to themselves before explaining it to other people. This knowledge will help them to feel convinced that what is being done is correct and that it is their own decision as well as that of the experts. Otherwise, they might easily feel that they are acquiescing to an intervention that is based on trial and error, which might prove to be all error. Here again, the concept of being sexually unfinished is invaluable, as are diagrams that illustrate how such a condition may appear (Figures 18 and 20). Many parents find it helpful to have copies of these diagrams to use when they talk with their relatives and others. Parents also are helped by having a brief written medical vocabulary with which to identify their child's anomalous condition—terms such as "hypospadias," "enlarged clitoris," "overactive adrenocortical glands," "incomplete labial fusion," and "hormonal insufficiency," for example. There is a magic about words and a power in technical terms that silences idle curiosity, for the idly curious hate to have their ignorance exposed. Medical terminology also enables a parent or an older patient to have the last word in any conversation, by telling the inquisitive one, if necessary, to satisfy his or her curiosity by speaking with a doctor.

The first people with whom the parents need to talk are their closest relatives, usually their own parents. They then usually explain their predicament to their siblings and a few very close friends. To deal with the larger community, they may enlist the cooperation of a more or less public figure who is connected to the family, such as a member of the clergy, a family doctor, a nurse, a counselor, a social worker, a teacher, or a lawyer, and give this person the facts of the situation. The family can authorize this person to explain the situation to other curious community members and, at the same time, request them to stop any gossip and to be honest about the situation for the sake of the child's future. Some parents have found that it is immensely helpful to show their baby, once the surgical correction has been accomplished, to a few key people, such as the baby-sitting parents who take turns caring for infants during church gatherings. Childcare providers and others who change the baby's diapers also need to be taken into confidence.

Those who are most likely to be overlooked at the time of a sex reannouncement are the older brothers and sisters of the baby. They, of all people, deserve an accurate explanation of their brother's or sister's having been born unfinished. Otherwise, they could logically reach the conclusion that a sex reannouncement could happen to them, too, with or without their permission. Parents are often too embarrassed or squeamish to talk straightforwardly with their older children, offering instead some platitudes about God's intentions or something similar. Therefore, one of the baby's health care team should talk to these older siblings if the parents are too inhibited to do so, and should certainly be available for consultation.

It will undoubtedly also be necessary for an informed professional, as the years pass, to be available to talk directly to the patient, now grown older. This consultant will be able to maintain a professional's impartiality, whereas the parents will perhaps be embarrassed, evasive, and, most important, unknowledgeable. As in other embarrassing situations involving sex, they can refer their child's difficult inquiries to the professional who, in turn, can open the channels of communication between parents and child through a joint session in which knowledge is shared and made explicit.

Direct and frank talk with the child is an absolute imperative when the possibility of changing the sex of rearing is raised, not in the neonatal period, but many years later when gender identity is so far advanced that it is irreversible. In this case, the issue is not that of sex reannouncement, but the far more complex one of sex reassignment.

10

Pubertal Hormonal Anomalies

In this chapter, the error, so-called, is in the timing of the onset of puberty—either too early or too late—and whether it matches or mismatches the child's sex as a boy or girl. In girls, the onset of puberty is expected from between the ages of 11 and 14, and, in boys, from 12 to 15, more or less. Nature does not always perform as expected, however. It is possible for puberty to begin as early as the 1st year of life, or to be delayed until the late teens or beyond.

PRECOCIOUS PUBERTY

When a girl shows the first signs of sexual development, at age 10 or even 9, the onset of puberty, although early, is generally considered to be within normal limits. The same is true of a boy whose puberty is first evident at age 11. Before these ages, the onset of puberty is considered precocious (Figure 36). Early puberty in many individuals can be explained as the result of a premature signal from the hypothalamic-pituitary biological clock, without any other pathology (Figure 37). In other cases, the early start of the pubertal clock is the secondary result of a tumor or other pathology in the hypothalamic-pituitary structures. The tumor or other lesion is not necessarily dangerous or fatal. Boys are more likely than girls to show tumor involvement as a cause of precocious puberty. Girls are more likely than boys to begin early pubertal development, especially at age 9 or younger, without any brain complications for the diagnostician to be concerned with. This uncomplicated condition, in both boys and girls, is named precocious puberty of idiopathic or central type, signi-

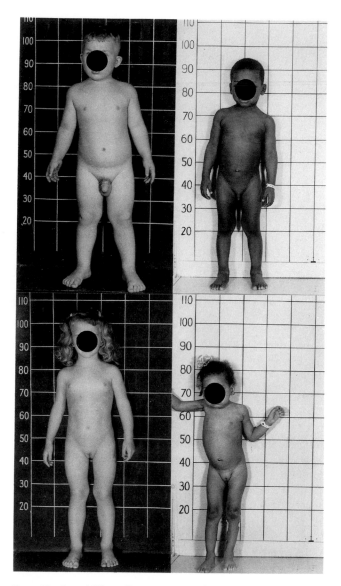

Figure 36. Four children, all age 2½ years. (Left top) a boy with early sexual maturation; (left bottom) a girl with early sexual maturation. (Right top) a typically developing boy; (right bottom) a typically developing girl.

fying that it originates centrally in the brain. This type of early puberty may run in families. For either sex, when puberty begins early, a complete diagnostic evaluation is in order to rule out the possibility of dan-

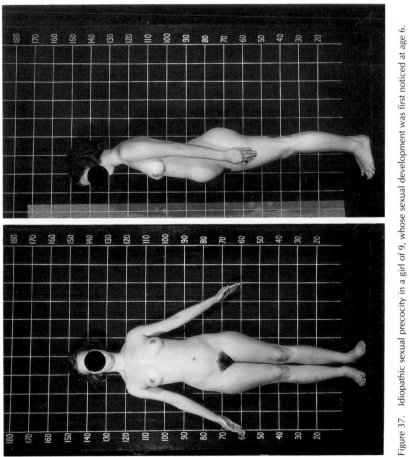

Figure 37. Idiopathic sexual precocity in a girl of 9, whose sexual development was first noticed at age 6.

71

gerous complications, especially a brain tumor, and to establish the benign diagnosis of idiopathic sexual precocity.

In boys, there is another form of early puberty that is triggered by masculinizing hormone from the adrenocortical glands, which are working in error (Figure 38). In 46,XY males this is congenital adrenal hyperplasia (CAH), the counterpart of which in 46,XX females produces hermaphroditism and, if untreated, precocious virilization, as discussed in Chapter 6. In boys with CAH, when hormonal replacement therapy with cortisol is given from infancy onward, early puberty is held in abeyance until normal puberty occurs at the proper age or possibly a little earlier.

In CAH syndrome in both boys and girls, the masculinizing hormone of puberty is produced by the adrenocortical glands independently of the biological clock of puberty. By contrast, in the central varieties of early puberty, as in normal puberty, the secretion of feminizing estrogen from the ovaries and masculinizing androgen from the testicles are both dependent on timing instructions from the biological pubertal clock. These instructions are carried to the gonads (the ovaries and testicles) by the two gonadotropic hormones, LH (luteinizing hormone) and FSH (follicle-stimulating hormone), which are secreted by the pituitary gland (see Chapter 8). A starter substance, LHRH (luteinizing hormone releasing hormone) is released from the hypothalamus, which tells the pituitary to release a combination of luteinizing hormone and follicle-

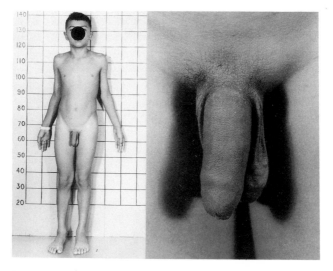

Figure 38. Early sexual maturation in a boy of 7 with untreated 46,XY congenital adrenal hyperplasia (CAH).

stimulating hormone. LHRH is released in pulses, not continuously. It is possible to slow down and stop the progress of puberty that begins too early by stopping these pulses of LHRH with an LHRH analog, a synthetic compound corresponding to LHRH.

Some children do not tolerate LHRH analog treatment and develop undesirable side effects. For some individuals, it is possible to fall back on an older form of treatment using either cyproterone acetate (Androcur) or medroxyprogesterone acetate (Depo-Provera), hormones that have a neutralizing effect on both estrogen and androgen, the puberty-producing hormones.

Both hormones are used in Europe, but only the latter has been officially approved for use in the United States. These hormones suppress the production of estrogen and androgen, but they do not slow bone growth and thus allow full growth in height. Depo-Provera is a multipurpose hormone: It is used also as a contraceptive hormone and, like Androcur, as an antiandrogen for the treatment of sex-offending paraphilias.

Even with medical intervention to slow down premature development, the management of precocious puberty relies heavily on sexological counseling and sex education. Sexological counseling seeks to reduce the disparities among chronological age, statural or physique age, and social age. Social age (including intellectual age and academic age), tends to develop parallel to chronological age and to be divorced from physique age. Because the physical size and energy of a pubertally precocious child permits his or her mixing with older and bigger children, social age may become advanced over chronological age. In fact, social age can, and should, be deliberately accelerated by academic advancement when possible, and by social and recreational inclusion with children 1 or 2 years older. In this way, the number of years is reduced in which the child exists in an uncomfortable position of disharmony between physical and social development.

The psychosexual age of children with precocious puberty synchronizes more closely with their overall social age than with either their physique age or chronological age. Thus, their manifested psychosexuality is not automatically determined by the degree of their pubertal maturation, but is in keeping with that of their playmates, friends, and acquaintances. In their erotic dreams and fantasies, the content of the imagery and ideas of bodily intimacy reflects their actual knowledge and their social age. Among the very young, for example, kissing and other scenes from television romances take precedence over scenes of copulation that typically remain unfamiliar until a later age. Pubertally precocious children do not constitute a menace as child molesters, as some uninformed adults have been known to fear. Those children who are reproductively fertile at an early age typically do not reproduce until the average age in their family and community.

PUBERTAL DELAY OR FAILURE

At the opposite end of the spectrum from precocious puberty is delayed puberty (Figure 39). The child who lags in reaching puberty at the normal age may be showing the first signs of chronic failure to commence puberty spontaneously, as has been discussed in connection with several syndromes. It is clearly important to establish the diagnosis and to distinguish the special conditions of impairment from the uncomplicated type of delay that may be simply a sign of "late blooming." Although it is a good general principle not to interfere when Nature will do the work

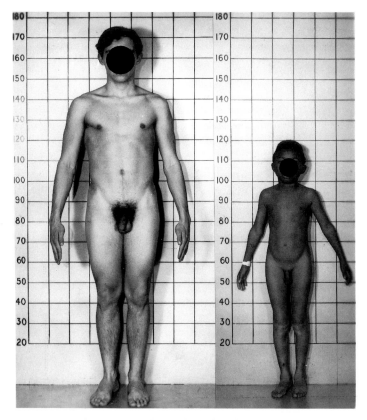

Figure 39.   Two boys age 17. Left, normal growth and maturation. Right, an extreme case of hypopituitary pubertal delay (before treatment) in a boy with retarded statural growth, both secondary to a deficiency of growth hormone from the pituitary gland.

unaided, there are limits on how long to wait for Nature. In the case of late blooming, when puberty is prolonged far beyond the early teens, the deleterious effect of physical infantilism on social and psychological maturation is ordinarily too great a risk to justify prolonged postponement of hormonal "starter" intervention. The treatment may be to prod the gonads into action with sex hormones or to imitate the triggering action of the pituitary on the gonads with gonadotropin. In either case, the treatment should be conservative, in deference to the remote possibility of injuring fertility. It is impossible to predict the degree of fertility risk, individually, especially in males. Many cases that may seem to be simply instances of late blooming will actually turn out to be more complex, and these individuals are destined to be infertile even without intervention to induce pubertal onset.

Chronic pubertal failure is more common in males than in females. The absence of puberty is sometimes primarily attributable to a deficit in the gonads themselves and sometimes to a deficit in the pituitary gland's gonadotropic stimulation of the gonads, with or without various other complexities. In either case, the long-term treatment is the same, namely, replacing the sex hormone that is missing. In boys, the result of treatment is a perfect imitation of Nature when the problem is attributable to the sex glands, but is frequently much less than perfect when the problem is with the pituitary gland, as several ancillary pituitary hormones may be involved. It is particularly difficult to get good growth of facial and body hair in an individual with a hypopituitary disorder. Consequently, the complexion often remains juvenile and is a source of embarrassment. The routine hormonal replacement dosage may need to be doubled for such individuals. For unexplained reasons, pituitary pubertal deficiency is much less common in girls than in boys.

The pituitary gland makes many hormones and it may fail to make only one of them, or more. If LH and FSH, the gonad-stimulating hormones, only are missing, then the individual's physical sexual maturation is affected, but not his or her statural growth. If growth hormone is also missing, the individual's sexual maturation will be accompanied by hypopituitary dwarfism, unless appropriately treated with synthetic growth hormone. If other pituitary hormones are missing or deficient, then various other conditions may be present, but they are infrequent. The missing hormones can be replaced.

One form of delayed puberty that is associated with retardation of statural growth, intellectual development, and social maturation is secondary to child abuse, neglect, and deprivation. This condition is referred to as psychosocial dwarfism and, more recently, as the Kaspar Hauser syndrome (Money, 1992). The effective intervention is to relocate the child to a new and favorable environment. Some catch-up growth, including the onset of puberty if delayed, is then possible, but the longer the period of abuse, the greater the amount of permanent impairment.

The psychological problem of pubertal delay or failure with attendant immaturity of appearance can be addressed by reducing, as much as possible, a discrepancy between chronological age and social age, despite the immaturity in physique age. The problem is particularly difficult when dwarfism is also present, for then the individual has the additional handicap of shortened height, to which people react unthinkingly, as though a person so short must still be socially a child.

The entire problem of psychological development in impaired pubertal development, even when it is treated, is made more complex by individual personality traits and psychodynamics. It is quite possible that some forms of pubertal failure carry a predisposition to psychopathology. This is the case in Klinefelter syndrome, discussed in Chapter 2. It is likewise the case in Kallmann syndrome, a condition of pubertal failure consequent on failure of the hypothalamus to produce LHRH to stimulate the pituitary, which in turn fails to stimulate the testicles. Kallmann syndrome can be traced to deletion of a gene inherited through the mother on the short arm (Xp22.3) of one of the child's X chromosomes. The gene is named KALIG-1 (Kallmann syndrome interval gene [Bick et al., 1992]). The same gene has a deleterious effect on the brain cells responsible for the sense of smell so that individuals with Kallmann syndrome are either partially or completely anosmic. The syndrome is more prevalent in males than females.

Some individuals with pubertal failure who also have severe personality disturbance do not improve after obtaining good somatic (physical) response to hormone replacement therapy. It is not uncommon to find people who so resent the indignity of their condition that they try to restore themselves to normality magically by denying the need for medical intervention and even by discarding their medication.

Conversely, there are other individuals who have the psychological capacity to have a dating and social life before intervention for their sexual immaturity, and who may even get married and perform coitally. Such people are examples of what self-confidence can do. Some individuals exemplify the little-known fact that sexual thoughts, images, and dreams, as well as being sexually arousing by visual and narrative materials, can be operational in a somatically juvenile male who has attained the age when the biological clock of hormonal puberty normally comes into action. The presence of androgen itself is not in all cases an absolute prerequisite for this aspect of eroticism. However, androgen greatly increases the frequency of sexuoerotic arousal, including its genitopelvic component, which, in some cases, is nonexistent without the hormone.

GYNECOMASTIA

Gynecomastia, or breast development in a male, is an anomaly of sex differentiation that has already been mentioned in connection with hermaphroditism. Gynecomastia also occurs in otherwise normal males, having its onset with puberty (Figure 40). Breast enlargement may be small, transient, and self-reducing or large, as in a pubertal girl, and irreversible except by surgery. It is a source of mortification to the boy concerned, unless by some extraordinary coincidence he also has a gender-identity disorder and wants to be a girl. Its deleterious psychological effects may be widespread and difficult to displace, even after successful plastic surgery. Sexological counseling should include reassurance that breast enlargement is not automatically a sign of other feminine traits or tendencies to come. The cause of gynecomastia is not fully known.

HIRSUTISM AND AMENORRHEA

Although the full process regulating hair growth and baldness has not yet been fully ascertained, it is known that androgen plays a major role in both hair growth and baldness. In males, androgen permits body hair to develop within the limits set by hereditary type. Females, if exposed to excessive amounts of androgen, will grow excessive body hair distributed in a masculine pattern. Figure 41 shows an extreme example of hir-

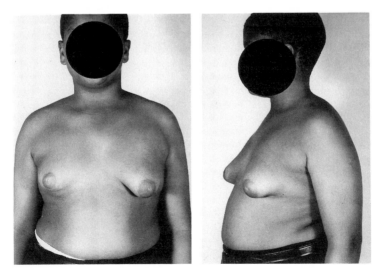

Figure 40.   Spontaneous breast development in a boy (gynecomastia) age 13 prior to corrective surgery.

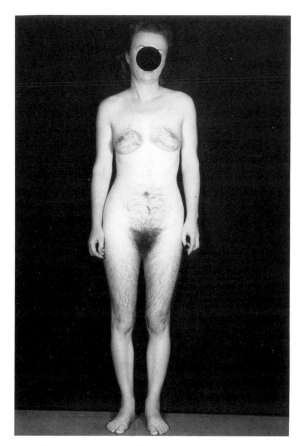

Figure 41. An extreme case of hirsutism produced by a masculinizing tumor of one of the adrenocortical glands.

sutism produced by a masculinizing adrenocortical tumor. Another
extreme example of hirsutism, an individual with untreated CAH syndrome with female hermaphroditism, is shown in Figure 42. Before the
discovery of cortisol treatment in 1950, girls with CAH syndrome grew
up to look like an exaggerated Mr. Atlas on a bodybuilding magazine
cover. With early cortisol intervention, that no longer happens. There are
lesser degrees of CAH hirsutism that have their onset not in childhood
but in adolescence or adulthood. These lesser CAH conditions can also be
relieved by cortisol therapy. Hirsutism itself is not invariably of androgenic origin. In some instances, it may be a hereditary trait.

The cortices of the adrenal glands are not always the abnormal
sources, as they are in CAH syndrome, of excess androgen. An abnormality of the ovary itself may be responsible. In Stein-Leventhal syn-

Figure 42. Masculine facial hair growth in a girl of 16 with untreated 46,XX congenital adrenal hyperplasia (CAH) syndrome of female hermaphroditism.

drome, one type of abnormal ovarian function, the ovaries are enlarged with cysts. The onset is postpubertal, usually in young adulthood. Women with Stein-Leventhal syndrome (also called polycystic ovary syndrome) develop amenorrhea, missing their periods at the same time as they become hirsute. Both symptoms can be relieved by a wedge-shaped surgical reduction of the enlarged ovaries, supplemented possibly with an antiandrogenic hormone to restore normal ovarian function. Menstrual failure usually accompanies an androgen excess that is severe enough to produce considerable hirsutism. There are, however, many other reasons for the absence of menstruation, including primary amenorrhea and functional or situational amenorrhea. Amenorrhea is a symptom of self-starvation in anorexia nervosa. Athletes in heavy training may develop amenorrhea as may dancers and fashion models who undereat.

It is much more difficult to get rid of hair growth than it is to induce it. A girl with excessive hair growth is best advised to opt for electrolysis, regardless of what help she may expect from hormone intervention or other intervention. In addition, she will generally need special counseling to help prevent serious disturbance of social and personality development.

Hirsutism, although it may be in part a genetic trait, is androgen-related in females as well as males. Androgen-induced hirsutism in girls is not accompanied by a corresponding masculinization of the gender identity or the body image. Therefore the woman with hirsutism is mortified and intent on ridding herself of the unwanted hairiness.

11

*Transpositions
of Gender Identity*

Without a second thought, most people simply take it for granted that a baby will grow up to have the gender identity and role (G-I/R) that agrees with the sex to which it is assigned at birth on the basis of the external genital appearance. Most people get by without a second thought because they assume that the different variables of sex converge in most individuals to be concordantly either all male or all female. Identify one variable, and you have identified them all, is the general rule.

Although this general rule does not apply to individuals with hermaphroditism, for these individuals there is a high incidence of concordance between the assigned sex and the G-I/R, especially when the surgical, hormonal, and social intervention has been directed toward concordance. There is no more dramatic example of how G-I/R agrees with assigned sex than when two individuals with the same diagnosis are differently assigned, one as a boy, and the other as a girl, and the G-I/R differentiates as masculine and feminine, respectively (Figure 43).

SEX REASSIGNMENT: FOR INDIVIDUALS
WITH BIRTH DEFECTS OF THE SEX ORGANS

In individuals with hermaphroditism and related birth defects, the gender-identity/role (G-I/R) may or may not develop to agree with idealized social stereotypes of masculine and feminine. Regardless of assigned sex, children whose prenatal and neonatal history included significant hormonal masculinization show behavioral development during the

81

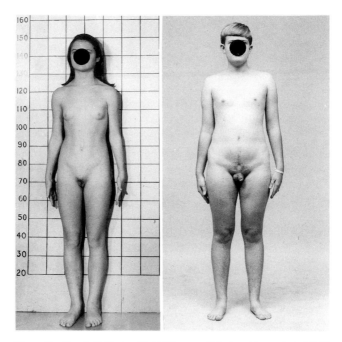

Figure 43. Two individuals with 46,XX congenital adrenal hyperplasia (CAH) syndrome of female hermaphroditism, but with different assignment, rearing, surgical repair, and hormonal regulation. Each has a gender identity and role to agree with rearing. Note the prosthetic testes in the boy (right).

juvenile years characterized by a high level of kinetic energy expenditure and by indifference to doll play and maternal rehearsal play. In girls, such behavior qualifies as tomboyish and in boys as boyish. Tomboyism is frequent, although not universal, in girls with CAH syndrome, and in some girls with a diagnosis of congenital male hermaphroditism or micropenis, or of neonatal loss of the penis (ablatio penis) in a circumcision accident.

Agreement between sex of assignment and G-I/R is not, however, a universal rule. The G-I/R may become established in repudiation or in partial repudiation of an assignment that the individual ultimately concludes was in error. The likelihood of reaching this conclusion is increased if, in cases of birth defect of the sex organs, the person has grown up stigmatized. Stigmatization takes place as a sequel to even subtle discrimination, at home, in the clinic, at school, or in the community. Discrimination may be solicitous and well meant, or rejecting and ridiculing. In the clinic, it is easy for a doctor's concern with pathology to be misconstrued by the patient as signifying that the entire self is pathological and no good. Similarly, parents may despise, criticize, and avoid the pathology in their child who, in turn, feels despised, criticized and avoided as a person.

Stigmatization may occur irrespective of diagnosis and of whether the sex of rearing has been as a boy or a girl. Thus, it is possible for two people with the same diagnosis each to repudiate the sex of rearing so that one is reassigned from male to female, and the other from female to male (Figure 44).

There are some individuals with birth defects of the sex organs in which the repudiation of the assigned sex is made not by the growing child, but by the parents and others called in as consultants. It may, however, be utterly impossible for the child to change the G-I/R that has differentiated in concordance with the assigned sex, no matter how logical the rationale for a reassignment of sex. Another child, by contrast, may have developed a G-I/R with sufficient wavering between masculine and feminine so that, with effective preparation and transitional support, a

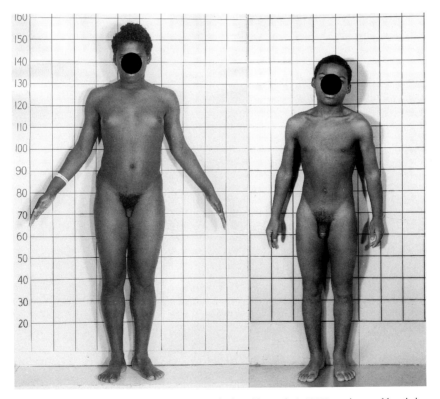

Figure 44.   Two individuals with 46,XX congenital adrenal hyperplasia (CAH) syndrome of female hermaphroditism. By age 12, each had elected a reassignment of sex. They are seen here after reassignment with hormonal regulation and before the sex organs of the girl (left) were surgically feminized.

sex reassignment may be considered. The rationale for such a change is that rehabilitation in the reassigned sex would permit coital adequacy in adulthood and perhaps reproductive fertility. On the basis of this rationale, it is intellectually and pragmatically rather satisfying to many health care providers as well as others if a female hermaphrodite assigned and ostensibly reared as a boy repudiates being a boy in favor of reassignment as a girl. Should the same individual repudiate her rearing as a girl, sex reassignment as a boy would not be intellectually so satisfying. Nonetheless, there is no point in insisting on continuing an unacceptable female assignment or on imposing a female reassignment if the end result would be psychological disaster. Moreover, the G-I/R might remain immutably masculinized, regardless of reassignment, and the erotic orientation would continue to be toward females. This situation would introduce a new and disputatious issue, namely lesbianism.

The same principle holds in the corresponding case of male hermaphroditism and male homosexuality. Erotic attraction toward males may be positively valued in certain individuals when sex assignment as a male is repudiated in favor of reassignment as a female. These are individuals in whom the penis will remain undeveloped and clitoral in size and coitally unfunctional in adulthood, whereas after surgical and hormonal feminization, the individual will be able to function with satisfaction as a female attracted to a male.

There is no more extreme quandary regarding sex reassignment than in an individual with total loss of the penis (ablatio penis). In some such individuals, the sex is reassigned and the child is raised as a girl. As a girl, the child's status is complicated by the parent's knowledge that they are rearing a child who once was a normal boy. Close relatives and neighbors share the same knowledge, which may be misused in a heartless, taunting way, especially among school children. In addition, the child may be cast in the role of hostage in a malpractice suit. All in all, it is a difficult situation, regardless of the sex of rearing.

The most expeditious rule to follow is that no child, after the toddler age, should have a sex reassignment imposed on the basis of a dogmatically held principle. Every person should be evaluated individually and sex reassignment considered on its own merits.

SEX REASSIGNMENT:
FOR INDIVIDUALS WITH GENITALS NOT MALFORMED

Whether elective or enforced, sex reassignment in individuals with hermaphroditism and related birth defects can generate considerable moral controversy, but not to the same extent as sex reassignment in individuals without congenital anomalies of the sex organs. Such cases are classified as transsexualism (American Psychiatric Association, 1994). The etiology of transsexualism is not known.

The crossover in transsexualism is from male to female (MF) (Figures 45 and 46) and from female to male (FM) (Figure 47). In both instances, the transsexual is a person who typically, although not invariably, is normal in body build and functioning according to the criteria of physiological tests and measurements. By contrast, sexopsychologically the transsexual is not an ordinary, but an extraordinary, person. No amount of literature review substitutes for direct personal contact with a transsexual in order to appreciate what it must be like to be one and to comprehend how fully transsexuals differ from nontranssexual men and women. Transsexual individuals have the body image of the other sex and are fixated, in the manner of a monomania, on changing their actual body to agree with their body image, and on living the role of the sex of the body image. In some individuals, the transsexual fixation has been present and unremitting since childhood, whereas in others it may be episodic until, later in life, it becomes permanent.

In some individuals, the transsexual body image and erotic orientation are concordant, and in others they are not. Without sex-reassignment surgery, a MF transsexual may live as a "lady with a penis," which may be the only possibility in some communities and in some parts of the world. If this lady with a penis is erotically attracted to males, legally and socially the attraction is defined as homosexual, whereas after hormonal and surgical sex reassignment it is redefined as heterosexual.

The reverse of this sequence occurs when, prior to hormonal and surgical sex reassignment, a MF transsexual is erotically attracted to females, and lives as a man who cross-dresses episodically. He may be unable to perform heterosexually without the erotic stimulus of being cross-dressed. He may be married and have fathered children. In midlife, for example, he may commence living full time as a woman and become hormonally and surgically sex reassigned. If erotic attraction toward females continues, then it is no longer legally and socially defined as heterosexual but homosexual, and the individual is looked upon, and perhaps self-defined, as a lesbian.

Psychotherapy has proved to be ineffectual in changing the body image fixation on sex reassignment in the fully developed syndrome of transsexualism. Amelioration of suffering due to the fixation is contingent on sex reassignment.

In MF sex-reassignment surgery, the skin of the penis is not detached from the body. It is used, possibly with part of the skin of the scrotum, to make a lining for the newly opened channel of the artificial vagina. The sexual sensitivity of this skin, together with other sensitive tissue in the genital area, ensures the continuance of pleasurable erotic

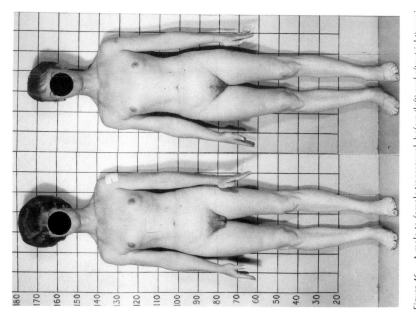

Figure 46. A male-to-female transsexual, before (left) and after (right) surgical reassignment as a woman. The breasts in this individual also developed as a result of female hormone therapy.

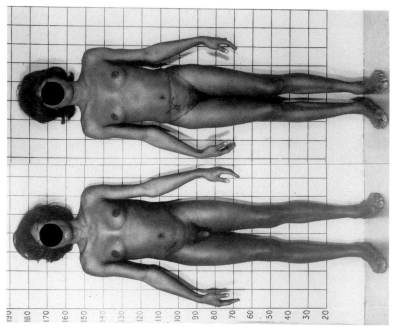

Figure 45. A male-to-female transsexual before (left) and after (right) surgical reassignment as a woman. The breasts developed as a result of female hormone therapy. On the right, a belt keeps the vaginal form in place.

86

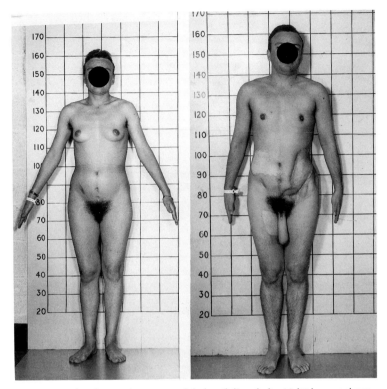

Figure 47. A female-to-male transsexual, before (left) and after (right) hormonal masculinization and surgery for breast reduction (mastectomy) and construction of a simulated, skin-grafted penis.

feeling, which is to some extent dependent on combined estrogenic and progestinic hormone replacement therapy. Some persons characterize this feeling as a satisfying glow that increases in strength and diffuses throughout the body. Others characterize it more as a peak or climax, possibly similar to the orgasm as formerly experienced and repudiated. Many persons, adhering to a stereotype of female sexuality, report that giving erotic satisfaction to a male partner genuinely outweighs self-satisfaction.

Female sex hormone therapy promotes breast enlargement in MF transsexuals. It does not feminize the voice and does not eliminate body or facial hair, for which electrolysis is necessary. Female sex hormone therapy does increase subcutaneous body fat, reduces the muscle mass, and decreases the oiliness of skin, notably of the face, in accordance with more feminine physical characteristics.

In FM sex reassignment, the breasts and internal female organs are removed. Externally the clitoris is preserved, and it is embedded into the base of an artificial penis that is constructed from a skin graft cut from the abdominal wall. The procedure is complex, requiring several operations before the tube of skin hangs down in the position of a penis, complete with a urinary tube. The penis constructed in this way cannot become erect, but needs to rest in some form of support to penetrate a partner's vagina. Orgasm is triggered from the region of the intact clitoris and is partly dependent on the continuance of male sex hormone therapy.

Male hormone therapy enlarges the vocal cords and masculinizes the voice. It increases the coarseness and distribution of body and facial hair, but induces loss of hair on the head if baldness is a family trait. The skin becomes more oily, and acne may appear. The clitoris responds by enlarging, but not sufficiently to allow surgical reconstruction as a penis.

All things considered, the outcome of FM genital reconstruction is technically less than satisfactory, not to mention the expense in money and time for multiple surgical interventions. Many FM sex-reassigned transsexual persons, although not all, can be satisfied genitally with wearing a genital prosthesis.

The term transsexualism signifies a method of rehabilitation (by changing sex) as well as a diagnosis. Sex reassignment is social as well as hormonal and surgical. Social rehabilitation involves family counseling, as well as legal and occupational counseling, and possibly community education as well.

The partners of postoperative transsexuals usually know the medical history of their mates. These partners may not have had contacts with homosexuals or the "gay" world. Many partners do not feel like homosexuals themselves. They judge their transsexual partners by their personality and behavior, not by their anatomical history or sterility. Some partners, by contrast, are specifically attracted erotically to transsexuals with or without surgical intervention.

TRANSVESTOPHILIA (FETISHISTIC TRANSVESTISM)

The dividing line between preoperative MF transsexualism and male transvestophilia, also known as fetishistic transvestism, is not clearcut. In the earliest phase, both conditions manifest the distinctive symptom of cross-dressing in female garments. In MF transsexuals, cross-dressing progresses, by definition, to a complete crossover, whereas in male transvestophilia there is no such progression. Nevertheless, in transvestophilia, cross-dressing persists, and the wearing of female garments is necessary for erotic arousal and sexual performance.

Although both men and women engage in cross-dressing, sometimes merely as a fashion statement, the fetishistic cross-dresser is typically, if not invariably, a male. The sexual orientation, as judged by the sex of the partner, may be heterosexual, homosexual, or bisexual.

Fetishism is a form of unusual or "kinky" sex and is scientifically known as a paraphilia, in which the paraphile's sexual arousal and performance depends on the fetish object or material. The fetish of the male with transvestophilia is, in particular, women's lingerie. If actually wearing it is suppressed, then the substitute is a "mental videotape" of doing so. In the coital scenario of the male with transvestophilia, he is transformed into a female who is wearing female garments, and the female partner often is transformed into a male.

The individual with male transvestophilia is not confined to being the impersonator of a female only for the performance of sexual intercourse, however. Dressing up in high fashion, and appearing and passing as a woman in public becomes a major preoccupation. It is more intensely exciting if the individual's wife or girlfriend participates as a female companion. There are extensive national and international cross-dressing networks and associations. Cross-dressing conferences and vacation gatherings can be a highlight of the social calendar.

The etiology of transvestophilia, as with that of transsexualism, remains to be discovered. Treatment for transvestophilia per se is not imperative, but secondary symptoms, such as anxiety attacks or depression, and side effects, including those affecting family members, may need intervention with either psychopharmacological medication or counseling, or both.

— 12 —

Copulatory Sex Impairments

The disabilities brought together in this chapter share in common the characteristic that they do not originate from a birth defect of the sex organs, but from a defect of later origin. The type of defect is variable, and so is the cause. In each instance it is a defect that interferes with the anatomy and physiology of the sex organs and with the efficacy of their function in sexual intercourse. In addition, these defects are responsible for symptoms and disabilities that are known to occur in other individuals who do not have an identifiable physical defect, in which case they are customarily defined as psychogenic. Thus these nonpsychogenic conditions promise to shed light, eventually, on fundamental principles involved not only in their own origins but also in the origins of their psychogenic counterparts.

ERECTILE DYSFUNCTION:
IMPOTENCE AND PREMATURE EJACULATION

Erectile dysfunction or impotence refers to a failure of sexual performance in males. It means inability either to obtain or to maintain an erection. Erectile dysfunction may occur before or after ejaculation. If ejaculation does occur, it is sudden and premature, and the penis loses its erection before the man or his partner is ready for it to do so.

Erectile failure may be an isolated symptom not associated with any known diagnostic condition, or it may be one among multiple symptoms of a disease such as sickle cell anemia, leukemia, diabetes mellitus, vascular disease, and multiple sclerosis, among others. It may also be a side effect of radiation treatment or of surgery for prostatic hypertrophy or cancer, and of various pharmacological substances, including chemotherapy for leukemia and medications prescribed for high blood pressure and some psychiatric conditions.

Erectile dysfunction in Peyronie's disease takes the form of a painful inability to achieve full penetration. This inability is due to severe curvature of the penis either sideways or downward. The curvature is secondary to the spontaneous formation of a plaque of tough, scar-like tissue in the shaft of the penis. The cause of plaque formation in Peyronie's disease is not known, and there is no fully effective cure.

In men with paraplegia, a spinal cord injury in which the lower half of the body is paralysed and numb, the spinal reflexes responsible for penile erection are deconnected from the sexual and erotic centers of the brain. It is possible for localized stimulation to produce an erection and ejaculation but without watching or touching the penis, the man does not know an erection or ejaculation has happened. Arousal from erotic imagery and ideation in the form of fantasies and dreams takes place in the mind and brain and is not able to traverse the spinal cord and stimulate the penis to produce an erection. Correspondingly, the same principle applies for a woman with paraplegia.

A male with paraplegia does not experience quite the same pangs of mortification through inability to satisfy the partner as does the man whose penis has been severed or injured in such a way that erotic feeling and erection are retained in the stump. One such injury is permanent fibrotic destruction of the spongy erectile tissue of the penis following an unexplained attack of priapism in which blood coagulates in the penis and prevents detumescence (Figure 48).

The man with localized penile injury or trauma, unlike the man with paraplegia, does not lose the feelings and sensations of genitopelvic sexual drive. For him the ego is wounded time and again by having to stop sexual play after achieving orgasm himself without having been able to penetrate the vagina so that the partner may also reach orgasm in the manner that they both long for.

One of the lessons to be learned for men from paraplegia is that the brain centers for erotic arousal work in concert with the spinal genitopelvic reflexes to produce an erection. The erection may fail if the messages from the brain become blocked and do not activate the genitopelvic reflexes. The blockage may be specific to the situation or to the partner. This type of erectile dysfunction is commonly referred to as psychogenic impotence. It may be resolved by sexological counseling of not only the individual, but also the couple.

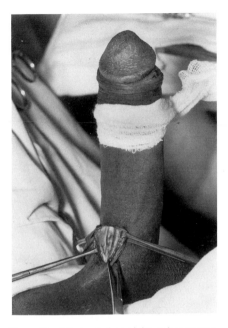

Figure 48. Priapism is the inability to lose an erection. It is painful and requires surgery, after which the ability to achieve an erection may be permanently lost.

PENETRATION PHOBIA

The female counterpart of impotence is penetration phobia. In the terminology of an earlier era, it was called frigidity. Phobia of penetration may express itself generally as erotic inertia and apathy which is, in some sexological texts, termed lack of or inhibition of sexual desire. It is more likely, however, that penetration phobia does not interfere with desire for the preliminaries of love play, but only with penovaginal intromission itself.

Penetration phobia may be so extreme as to manifest itself as a temporary, involuntary, scissors-like locking of the legs, making intercourse impossible. Penetration phobia may also be manifest as an extreme and painful dyspareunia, which is a spasm that so tightens the muscles surrounding the vaginal orifice that entry of the penis is impossible. More usually, penetration phobia manifests itself as an inability to enjoy intravaginal sex and an inability to build up to the climax of orgasm.

Like erectile dysfunction, penetration phobia may be an isolated symptom not associated with a known diagnostic condition, or it may be one of multiple symptoms of another condition such as a congenital defect, a defective repair of tissue torn while giving birth, a neoplastic growth, multiple sclerosis, or, probably the most common of all, localized infection. Penetration phobia may also be a side effect of medication. As in erectile dysfunction, penetration phobia may be specific to a situation or partner and thus be termed psychogenic. In that circumstance, sexological counseling is in order for the couple as well as the individual. Whether in males or females, situational or partner-specific dysfunction may be conceptualized as resisting or fighting with the sex organs. Individuals with this type of sexual dysfunction, however, are not able to recognize that there is a connection between the sexual symptom and the source of the ongoing conflict, although they do recognize, separately, the symptom and the conflict.

LOSS OF SEX ORGANS

Traumatic accident or surgical intervention may be responsible for varying degrees of impairment of sexual and erotic function as a sequel to impairment of the reproductive anatomy. In the male, loss of the testicles entails permanent sterility and, without hormone replacement therapy, loss of testicular androgen. Without androgen, ejaculatory fluid, chiefly from the prostate gland, fails to be secreted so that only a dry orgasm occurs. Erection is able to occur on the same basis as before puberty, but the frequency of erection diminishes, as does also the subjective experience of sexual drive.

In the male, surgical or radiological loss of part or all of the prostate gland may be necessary for treatment of prostatic enlargement, which may be either benign or malignant. Preservation of sexual and erotic functioning varies according to the magnitude of nerve fiber destruction, and is unpredictable ahead of time.

The external sex organs of the female, being less exposed than those of the male, are less at risk for injury. Some women, however, do require radical removal of the skin around the entire vulval area because of skin cancer. These women do not necessarily lose their sexual feelings, although they may discontinue sexual relations through fear of injury.

In individuals with hermaphroditism assigned and living as females, it is usual to perform surgery to remove or reduce an enlarged, masculine-looking clitoris. Radical clitoridectomy, however, with or without extirpation and closure of the entire vulva (infibulation) is a form of ritual female circumcision (see Chapter 7) performed on girls in a large part of Africa, especially in the northeast, and in southern Arabia (Lightfoot-Klein, 1989). As a ritual it is the counterpart of circumcision in boys and is without medical or scientific justification. Despite the importance of the clitoris as a focus of erotic feeling, its removal does not inevitably abolish the capacity to reach orgasm. There is no scale on which to measure any change in the intensity of erotic gratification, however.

Vulnerability of the internal female organs is evident from the incidence of diseases of the uterus and resultant hysterectomy. Some surgeons are far more conservative than others in undertaking this operation, and some are more attentive to the psychological preparation of their patients for the loss of an organ by which their biological purpose in the world is defined. Hysterectomy, provided the ovaries are left intact, does not impair the internal hormonal rhythm of the body, although menstruation can no longer occur. Hysterectomy does not directly impair sexual desire and response, including orgasm, but it may do so indirectly as a result of an adverse reaction to the actual loss of the uterus, or to undue postsurgical and irreversible contraction of the vault of the vagina.

13

A Counseling Guide

There are some questions and issues in counseling that arise not in connection with one syndrome alone, but are common concerns in several syndromes involving birth defects of the sex organs and, indeed, in many other psychoendocrine syndromes as well (Money, 1994a,1994b). The following topics are recurrent and need to be addressed for virtually every individual.

HEREDITARY TRANSMISSION

The personal subjective trauma of having produced an atypical baby is not necessarily experienced in the same way by every parent. Therefore, when advising couples, it is necessary to provide each of them with an opportunity to talk alone, as well as together. It is virtually universal for a mother to blame herself for any pregnancy that produced a less than "perfect" child, regardless of her empirical knowledge and intellectual sophistication. A father may also experience self-blame.

Although blame of the other parent rarely surfaces overtly, it may take its toll covertly. Eventually this blaming of the other may be responsible for deterioration of the marital relationship into an adversarial relationship, possibly culminating in separation and divorce. One warning signal is deterioration of the couple's sex life. Therefore, it is extremely desirable to provide each parent with an opportunity to talk about having produced an atypical baby and what effect this might have on their current sexual functioning. Apprehensions about genetic transmission and the possibility of having another baby with a sexual disability may be countered rationally, with etiological and genetic explanations. However, rationality alone does not resolve the sometimes pervasive and persistent traumatic effects of being less than a genetically perfect parent.

Probability statistics are of little value to a mother or father who wants to know if her or his next baby will have the same syndrome. Advice about the wisdom of attempting a new pregnancy requires considerations not only of probability statistics, but also of the morbidity risk specific to the syndrome and of the therapeutic prognosis. The possibility of prenatal diagnosis with the option of abortion or, as is sometimes possible, intrauterine treatment of the fetus should also be a consideration for a future pregnancy. For instance, prenatal glucocorticoid therapy is a possibility for a fetus with CAH syndrome. Anything that medical technology has to offer, however, is contingent on the personal, religious, and ethical concerns and obligations of the individuals involved, as well as on practical concerns, such as insurance coverage, and on pragmatic logic. Some people are reckless gamblers with fate, and some are cautious and insure themselves against it. The person responsible for genetic counseling should not attempt to dictate the actual decision about a new pregnancy. If he or she does, and if the couple do not comply, or if they have an unplanned pregnancy, they may feel too guilty or ashamed to see the counselor again for whatever further help they may need.

There are some syndromes in which hereditary transmission affects not only the immediate family but the larger kinship—for example, CAH syndrome and androgen insensitivity syndrome. Some families are extremely secretive about having a child with a sexual birth defect and impose censorship on how much information is disclosed even to siblings. In these families, the parents may be unable to talk straightforwardly even with affected offspring who, in turn, may not be in a position to share confidences, as adults, with siblings.

When relatives do not know that they might carry the gene for a syndrome already in the family, they are unable to plan properly for future pregnancies and pregnancy testing. If they do have genetic information, they know ahead of time exactly what to expect should they have a baby with the same birth defect of the sex organs as their relative. Knowing the diagnosis and what to do about it from the time of delivery onward can be invaluable in treatment.

Young couples who know they are at risk of producing progeny with disabilities are wisely counseled to be sure that they have adequate healthcare coverage before the pregnancy. If they do not, medical expenses may spell financial ruin, and they should be aware of whatever options are available to them.

INFERTILITY

Among the syndromes associated with birth defects of the sex organs are some in which infertility is guaranteed, others in which it is virtually certain, and still others in which fertility is a possibility. Withholding information from children and adolescents in order to "spare them" is an outdated policy, but it still exists. This approach is not only ethically dubious, but also rarely successful. In a hospital, as at home, the walls proverbially have ears. Children do overhear even without eavesdropping and, not infrequently, if left alone in an examining room are able to read sections of their medical charts. What they pick up incompletely and inadvertently can be more damaging than knowing the full story, which can be told not brutally, but with sensitivity. In this way, the truth can be incorporated into the play and fantasy that, in childhood, serves as rehearsal for the future. The traumatic shock of a sudden disclosure later is thus avoided.

It is unnecessarily heartless and blatantly untrue to express statements such as "You can't have any children," when having children by adoption or marrying a partner who already has children are obvious possibilities. Even if the chances of fertility are negligible, it is better to make a probability statement rather than an outright prophesy, for one never knows what new scientific advances may bring. For example, not very many years ago it was not possible, as it now is, to tell a girl who has a uterus but no ovaries about pregnancy by means of *in vitro* fertilization of a donated egg. This possibility exists irrespective of diagnosis and chromosomal status. In addition, a girl without a uterus also has the possibility of receiving a donated fertilized egg and bearing an ectopic pregnancy within the abdominal cavity. An abdominal pregnancy was experienced by a woman who became pregnant after having had a hysterectomy. A fertilized egg survived the operation and attached itself to the outer wall of the small intestine where it formed a placenta and amniotic sac and grew into a healthy female baby, delivered by cesarean section (Jackson, Barrowclough, France, & Phillips, 1980). Hope, even if it does not materialize, is a powerful beacon on the road to health.

Boys with a prognosis of infertility may, like girls, be told of parenthood by adoption, or by marrying and becoming the stepfather of an "instant family." They have also the possibility of relying on a sperm bank for donor insemination of their wives or partners.

Infertility allows another option, that of concentrating full time on an extradomestic career. This option appeals especially to some individuals with a prenatal history of hormonal masculinization, a neonatal history of female sex assignment, and a postnatal history of tomboyish energy expenditure and indifference to maternal rehearsal play. Some 46,XX CAH women fall into this category, and so also do some 46,XY women with a diagnostic history of congenital micropenis or male hermaphroditism.

CHROMOSOMAL AND GONADAL STATUS

After the technique of chromosome counting was developed in the 1950s, the extraordinary range of sex-chromosome genotypes that was compatible with both a male and female body form or phenotype meant that it was no longer feasible to equate XY exclusively with male and XX exclusively with female. Instead, it became necessary to specify an individual's chromosomal type. This is good news for 46,XY girls and women who no longer need to feel chromosomally stigmatized as males in some occult or mystical way. The same may be said for the smaller number of 46,XX boys and men. In childhood, 46,XY girls may fall back on the fictional idea that their Y chromosome is like an X with an arm broken off, and totally incapable of doing Y work. Instead of only talking about chromosomes, they should also see a picture of them (see Figures 4 and 5 for examples).

In the same manner, it is necessary to remove the stigma of the names of the sex glands (gonads), testes (or testicles) and ovaries, when they are discordant with an individual's being. In the annals of hermaphroditism, there are relatively few individuals living as men with a history of having been born with ovaries, but a relatively larger number of women with androgen insensitivity syndrome (AIS) have a history of having been born with feminizing testes.

There is no way that the words *ovaries* and *testes* can be expunged from a patient's medical chart, and no way of guaranteeing that patients will not ascertain their congenital gonadal status. What they need, therefore, is guidance in how to interpret what they ascertain. It is helpful to begin with diagrams of the embryo (Figures 18 and 20) to explain the bipotential nature of the cells that usually become either testes or ovaries and that sometimes do not. The inclusive or bipotential term is gonads, or sex glands. These terms maintain self-respect when an individual must make a diagnostic disclosure, for example, when filling out a medical questionnaire or during a medical examination with an unfamiliar doctor or nurse, or when revealing one's medical history in confidence to a friend or lover.

It is not possible to guarantee that information about an individual patient's chromosomal and gonadal status can be kept concealed. Moreover, under the Freedom of Information Act, patients have access to their own records. Wisdom dictates that the information be given thera-peutically before it escapes and becomes traumatizing.

SEXUAL INSTRUCTION

Sexual information must be available to all children. Sexual information, especially tailored to their circumstances, is an absolute must for all chil-dren with a sex anomaly of the body. Left to themselves to play, all infants and children tend to rehearse in play, as do macaque monkeys and other primates, the component acts of the total mating response. In monkeys, total deprivation of play, including sexual rehearsal play, results in severely aberrant mating behavior in adolescence and adult-hood, usually with total failure to breed successfully. If pregnancy is achieved, then mothering is grossly defective, so much so that the infant monkey perishes.

It is scarcely possible to envisage the social acceptance of copulation games in kindergartens in the near future. Therefore, adults must substi-tute with words the sex education lessons that children would otherwise spontaneously learn for themselves were they not exposed to the restraints and taboos of convention. Deeds must be replaced with words, if children are to know the truth about the role of their bodies in the reproduction of their kind, as well as the necessary sense and freedom of gender identity to be able to put this truth into practice in adulthood.

The sex education story that I have found effective over the years I tell step-by-step along with illustrative diagrams (Figures 49–54). The amount of information revealed at any one time depends on the age and interest of the child and the frequency with which one sees him or her. As long as they are not squeamishly evasive and inhibited, parents can gauge how much to tell at any one time, and they are always available for an added installment.

The tale begins with the baby egg, without a shell and no bigger than the dot made by the point of a pencil (Figure 49). This baby egg is released from the ovary and is then propelled along the tube into the baby nest (Figure 50). The egg is able to start growing into a baby only when it is joined by a sperm, which is made by the father. Three hundred million sperms all have a swimming race, wiggling their long propelling tails, trying to reach the egg (Figure 51). There is only one winner! The prize is to join the egg and grow into a baby. The winner burrows its head into the soft wall of the egg and drops off its tail. At this point, the egg travels down the uterine tube and fixes itself onto the wall of the uterus or baby nest (Figure 50). There it shares the mother's blood, in which liquid food and air are transported. The connecting tube enters the baby

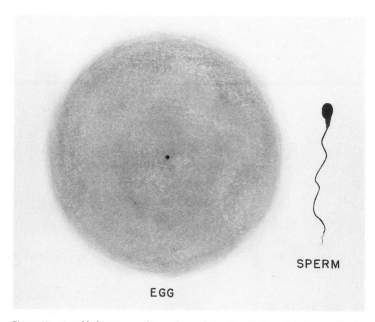

SPERM

EGG

Figure 49. A real baby egg is no bigger than a dot made with the point of a pencil in the middle of this drawing. A real sperm is so small that it cannot be seen without a microscope.

at the navel. There the egg grows, the limbs bud, and the organs form, until the baby is ready to be born (Figure 52). It gets pushed out down the baby tunnel or canal. The head comes out first so that the shoulders can be tucked close to the body (Figure 53).

Sperms are made in the father's testicles, which are really sperm factories. Sperms have to swim away from the testicles, through a long tube inside the body, and out through the penis (Figure 54). The penis stands up stiff and straight so that it can fit into the baby tunnel, where the sperms in their swimming liquid are pumped out to give them a good start on their swimming race and to make sure that they have a fair chance of finding the egg far up inside the baby nest. Sperms are so small that a pencil point is too big to draw one. The illustration in Figure 49 shows a super, giant-size, instead of a real, life-size sperm. You can see a real sperm only if you have a microscope to magnify it.

Parents hear this story not only so that they also can tell it to their children, in installments for the very young, but also so that they can retell it to children who forget, as children often do. Telling the story this way solves the problem of terminology, for medical terms can be added later, when children are older. For many parents, terminology has proved the biggest single stumbling block to effective communication

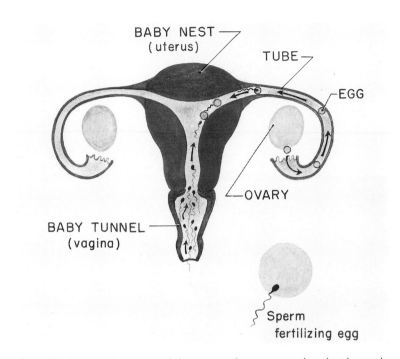

BABY NEST
(uterus)

TUBE

EGG

OVARY

BABY TUNNEL
(vagina)

Sperm
fertilizing egg

Figure 50.   Sperms swim up to search for an egg, and an egg moves along the tube searching for a sperm. The winner sperm fertilizes the egg.

with young children on matters of reproduction. With this stumbling block removed, child and parent can stay in mutual long-term contact on matters of sexual behavior and on what may be called the psychology and sociology of sex as distinguished from the physiology of sex. During early childhood, education in the sociology of sex means, among other things, advice on where and when to talk about the physiology of sex. The recommendation of keeping it a family and medical secret reserved for "your mommy and daddy and your doctor" is a simple expedient that prevents social embarrassment for parents at the dinner table, in the neighborhood, and elsewhere.

Adolescence is the age during which the sociology and psychology of sex and falling in love are preeminent in sex education. It is, therefore, in the sex education of the adolescent that parents reap the greatest reward for having kept open the channels of mutual confidence with early frankness.

In situations where open communication breaks down, the responsibility lies with adults to break the ice of silence. It is not enough to follow the maxim, "Answer your children's questions truthfully when they ask them," because the child who has frozen up will avoid asking any

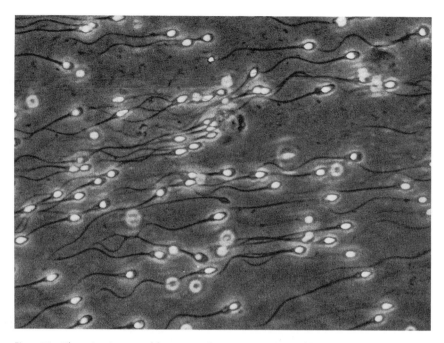

Figure 51.   The swimming race of the sperms. There are 300,000,000 of them—but only 1 winner.

questions at all. One way to break the deadlock is to use the technique of the parable to tell a story of a child in a similar predicament, who finally developed enough confidence to tell and ask about sexual matters. The parable technique (discussed in the following chapter) makes sure that a child knows that he or she is not unique or alone, and, above all, it ensures that the child knows the adult can listen to sex talk without exploding.

Pubertally precocious children need to know at least one person to whom they can bring any topic of their sexual experience or curiosity at any time. Typical adolescents have their own age-mates from whom they learn and find reassurance about teenage sex, but the child who develops precociously has no pubertal age-mates to act as sources regarding romantic feelings, dating, involvement with older teenagers, parental discipline, masturbation, and sexual identity. Children with precocious puberty respond very well to counseling and guidance. They display the same range of balance and common sense as do most adolescents during normal puberty. Ultimately, their contemporaries catch up with them, and they are no longer conspicuous, except that, especially in the case of boys, they are noticeably short-statured in adulthood. In their early years, the bones of children with precocious puberty grow and mature so rapidly that there is not time for them to grow tall.

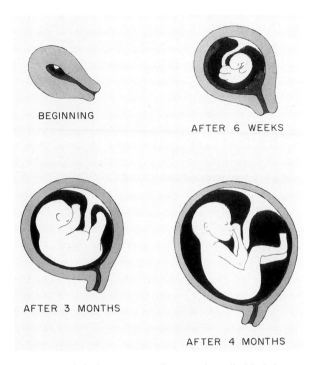

BEGINNING

AFTER 6 WEEKS

AFTER 3 MONTHS

AFTER 4 MONTHS

Figure 52.   A baby begins as a small spot on the wall of the baby nest (upper left). It is connected to the wall with the cord that brings nourishment from the mother through the baby's navel or belly button. After 4 months, it is 120 mm and weighs 110 gm (lower right).

Sex education for children with a birth defect of the sex organs needs to address the additional concerns of their self-image and their uncertainties about being seen nude by age-mates and others, concerns about future prospects of fertility and marriage, about impediments to sexual performance, and about how much to divulge to a future lover. As teenagers, their morale will benefit from a positive endorsement of a beginning sex life, rather than an excess of moralistic restriction. Sexual failure and partner rejection bring on despair.

Some parents provide their teenagers with sexual privacy at home in order to reduce the stress of secrecy and to demonstrate approval. One benefit of this policy is that it gives the parents themselves greater freedom from secrecy and silence in conducting their own sex lives. Contrary to the fears of some, it does not encourage younger siblings to be sexually active too soon, for every youngster has his or her own developmental timetable for becoming sexually active. Sexual emancipation in one's own home also has the very great advantage of encouraging a lasting one-to-one relationship as a defense against HIV/AIDS.

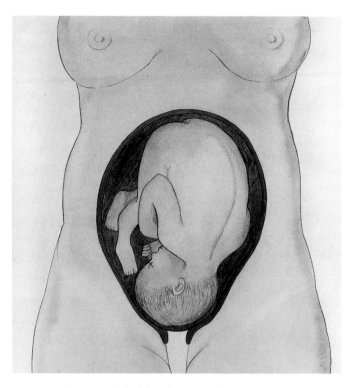

Figure 53.   After 9 months the baby is born. It usually comes out head first with its arms tucked at its sides.

SELF-KNOWLEDGE

What young people do not know, and the half-truths they formulate as a result, can be far more terrifying than knowing the truth. Most children hate being excluded from what the doctor tells their parents. As their ability to comprehend progressively matures, they have the right to know about their own medical history, the nature of their condition, and what to expect from intervention. The information can and should be worded so that it is therapeutic, not traumatic. A positive presentation includes terminology suitable for satisfying the curiosity of their age-mates as well as adults. There is need even for terminology to provide a superficial explanation of why it was necessary to miss school in order to keep a clinic appointment.

From the viewpoint of a child, hospital tests and procedures, especially those that appear arbitrarily imposed without explanation, may be experienced as the nosocomial (associated with a hospital or clinic) equivalent of abuse. Routine genital examinations and exposure are especially likely to fall into this category, particularly if there are medical-

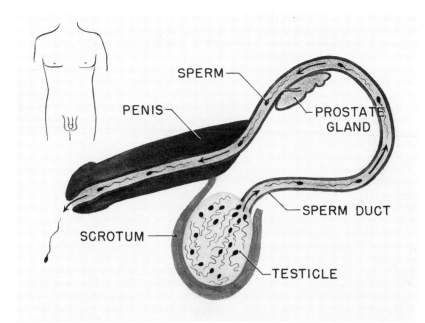

Figure 54. Sperms are made in the testicles. They swim and stay alive in the fluid made in the prostate gland. They are pumped out through the penis, which swells up with blood until it is firm enough to fit the vagina.

student bystanders. If exposure of the genitals or genital play at home or school has been forbidden and perhaps punished, the hospital examination is all the more gruesome and upsetting. Postoperatively, genital surgery also may seem like a form of abuse. No matter how erroneously misconstrued, the long-term effects of what is experienced as nosocomial abuse may be severe and lifelong. The impact of the experience may be ameliorated by counseling and prior explanation of the genital procedure, and preparation for it, including perhaps viewing a video demonstration of what to expect.

A birth defect of the sex organs, if known publicly, puts a child at risk for teasing and ridicule. Maintained as a secret, with absolutely no one to confide in, it may become an intolerable burden of despair. The child may need help in finding someone who is trustworthy in whom to confide. The confidant may be a brother or sister, another relative, or a friend. The value of such a person is not only as a confidant, but also as a mediator in case of accident or medical emergency, as someone who can provide necessary and possibly lifesaving diagnostic information.

For some children with a history of birth defect of the sex organs, there are associated symptoms or disabilities that impede their social acceptance by age-mates. Some children, for example, are excluded on the basis of very short stature. As mentioned earlier, because their height age is incongruent with their chronological age, they are infantilized by other people, adults and children alike, so that their social age hovers somewhere between height age and chronological age. If they are informed about the discrepancy between their three ages, they may be able to contribute significantly to advancing their social age. At the same time, family members and the larger community also may be able to become aware and stop at least some of the infantilization.

Occasionally, a 46,XY child with a history of micropenis, with or without the hermaphroditic complication of hypospadias, will have multiple additional congenital defects. One syndrome has become known by the acronym CHARGE (Money & Norman, 1988). In this syndrome, there are various neurological, sensory, and motor impairments, and also specific learning disabilities that affect not only academic learning, but social learning also. Because they have a social disability, children with CHARGE syndrome are likely to be ridiculed and shunned by their age-mates. So that they may maximize their potential, academic and recreational intervention is indicated.

Syndrome-specific disability calls for intervention in various other syndromes also, as discussed earlier with respect to Turner and Klinefelter syndromes. An unfortunate and totally unnecessary common experience of children with specific cognitive and social disabilities is that they are held personally responsible and blamed for their disabilities. Children with disabilities are greatly relieved to encounter nonjudgmental professionals who put blame fairly and squarely where it belongs, namely on the syndrome and not the person.

As mentioned earlier, in some individuals with hermaphroditism and related birth defects and syndromes, the G-I/R may not develop in agreement with the idealized social stereotypes of masculine and feminine. In the juvenile years, tomboyism in girls does not change in response to criticism, chastisement, or discipline. It may bring social ostracism from within the peer group from both girls and boys. The tomboyish girl has little or no interest in sedentary pursuits and would rather join in energetic team sports, gymnastics, and athletics. In late adolescence and adulthood, it is possible that a girl with a history of birth defect of the sex organs may fail the chromosome test required for sports competition. However, the test is under attack and may soon be abolished.

In adolescence, the tomboyish girl may or may not experience same-sex romantic and sexuoerotic attraction and establish a love affair with another woman. If she is socially defined as a lesbian, she may experience rejection by family, church, and the heterosexual community. The girl with a sexual anomaly may greatly appreciate knowing that her feelings and desires are attributable to her syndrome, and are not a matter of personal voluntary responsibility and moral choice.

The counterpart of the tomboyish girl is known rather pejoratively as the sissy boy, for which a better term is gender cross–coded boy. Among children with a history of birth anomalies of the sex organs, the proportion of those assigned and reared as males who grow up gender cross-coded may be smaller than their counterpart, tomboyish girls, but firm statistics are lacking. Among males born without anomalies of the sex organs, those who grow up gender cross-coded have a high probability of being romantically and sexuoerotically attracted in adulthood to a male in a same-sex relationship (Green, 1986; Money & Russo, 1979). Homosexual attraction may occur also in those with a history of gender cross-coding and of sexual birth defect. Boys with sexual anomalies, like girls, are relieved of a burden of self-blame and guilt by knowing to attribute homoerotic attraction to their syndrome, not to personal moral choice.

TEENAGE AUTONOMY AND SEXUALITY

Two of life's great assignments come to the foreground in the teenage years: autonomy and sexuality. Sexuality includes falling in love, and autonomy includes preparing for work and economic independence. Autonomy sometimes gets in the way of clinical compliance. Problems of compliance can exist at any age, but in infancy and childhood, the responsibility for compliance really lies with an adult caregiver. In teenage years, responsibility for compliance becomes progressively transferred to, or demanded by, the individual. Teenage noncompliance may be an example of the principle of inexistence, a magical belief that not taking medication signifies not being sick. When the medication is a sex hormone, noncompliance may also signify repudiation of becoming sexually mature, repudiation of genital desire as sexual sinfulness, or repudiation of the individual's hormonally induced status as male instead of female, or female instead of male.

It is not too far-fetched to say that in the United States teenage sex is widely regarded not only as an evil, but also as an epidemic. Teenagers and adults mutually recognize the communication wedge that splits them asunder on this issue. Unable to dislodge this wedge, some teenagers with a history of genital ambiguity are unable to confide not only in adults but also in their age-mates. Except perhaps in the clinic, they have no one with whom to share their romantic and erotic dreams, dreads, and apprehensions, such as when and how much to reveal to a boyfriend or girlfriend, or what to expect from sexual intercourse. For a comprehensive guide on how to be "the complete interviewer" and sexological counselor, the specialist reader is referred to *Reinterpreting the Unspeakable* (Money, 1994b).

14

The Parable Technique

The parable technique is a way of circumventing a communication impasse. The counselor narrates a story derived from a history of a person of the same age and with the same diagnosis as the patient. The story may also be derived from a composite of case histories. The topic of the story is presumed to apply to the listener who, even if electively mute, ascertains that the narrator is an informed listener with whom it is safe to reopen the topic at a later date. The parable technique is suitable for topics such as the timing of the onset of hormone replacement therapy and the timing of reconstructive genital surgery. The parable technique applies also to such touchy subjects as diagnostic self-knowledge, particularly about chromosomal and gonadal sex; masturbation; paraphilic erotic imagery and ideation; wet dreams; bisexual or homosexual attraction; ideas of sex change; impaired or defective genital function in sexual intercourse; sterility; fertility; pregnancy; revealing to a lover the prognosis of sterility; hereditary transmission; telling siblings and others about the possibility of future transmission; fear of rejection; lovesickness; and suicide. The parable technique is an effective approach for discussion of these topics with individuals with sex anomalies, their parents, siblings, and others significant in the lives of such individuals.

The great advantage of the parable technique is its nonjudgmentalism. The technique does not require the listener either to admit or to deny the relevance of a given topic, but simply indicates that the topic is safe to talk about and to be listened to.

In using the parable technique, the agenda is fixed but the inquiry is open-ended and spontaneous. Open-endedness allows the respondent the freedom to define the topic in terms of what it means to him or her personally. Subsequently, the inquiry becomes less open-ended, until eventually each particular topic may be closed with an interrogatory, employing forced-choice questions. Such questions are designed to get specific responses to specific details of chronology, prevalence, location, frequency, and measurement, for example.

An open-ended inquiry may be as straightforward as an announcement of the next topic on a standardized schedule of inquiry, for example, "Play—tell me about your child's play." This straightforward approach is based on the premise that the topic is in the public domain and poses no threat of stigmatization, self-incrimination, or breach of confidentiality.

In some instances it is necessary to specify, not assume, that a topic is indeed in the public domain, although it may be partly in the private domain. An example of an inquiry into such a topic is, "The bombing of abortion clinics has been in the news recently," or, "The gay pride parade was on the television news last week." If the respondent indicates familiarity with this news, it is then feasible to inquire as to his or her ideas about it. On this basis, it becomes feasible to lead the inquiry into more personal references concerning past history and future prospects regarding abortion or sexual orientation, for example.

The parable technique is especially valuable when a topic is not in the public domain but is taboo-ridden and potentially stigmatizing and self-incriminating.

The sportscaster's technique of a detailed play-by-play account is the approach to employ when the informant is recounting a personal experience or encounter. Otherwise, the account becomes too global and diffuse. In particular, if the account involves an adversarial relationship, the raw data can become lost in the inferential attribution of motivation and intent and in the subtle attempt to win the interviewer as an ally, or a favorable juror against the adversary. To establish maximum impartiality, one should interview the adversary, who also should adopt a play-by-play technique of reporting. Impartiality is enhanced and mutual understanding is increased if statements are not formed in a way that implies judging, preaching, or teaching. The maxim for everyone is: Don't judge, preach, or teach; just tell. Tell always about yourself and your own responses and subjective reactions. In order to best reveal the thoughts, images, and reactions of your innermost self, begin each statement with "I."

A classic example of the use of the parable technique, which is detailed below, dates back more than 30 years to one of the first occasions of the use of this technique. This technique was used with a boy with congenital micropenis (Money, 1991). When he was 10 years old, the following entry in his psychohormonal chart was made (Money, 1991).

At the outset of the interview, he said that he had asked for the appointment because he wanted to talk to me, but that he had nothing special to report or to ask. Pursuing a cue given me by the father, I took up the topic of his having done well academically in fourth grade, just completed, but perhaps not so well socially with other boys. In his usual candid way, he said that he doesn't go off with the other boys to play, but usually joins in the girls' group. There was a certain amount of face-saving: The girls wanted to have some boys with them, and they played the same games as boys play, like softball and handball. He wasn't the only boy in the group. He mentioned specifically his friend, a diabetic, whom the other boys don't want to bother with, because he can't run fast enough. He himself can run fast enough, but for him the other boys are too rough, always fighting, and he doesn't like to fight....He gave no evidence of attraction toward girls' toys, clothes, or domestic activities.

I decided to probe further into the significance of recreational alignment with girls by using the parable technique, namely, a narration of situational relevance used as a personalized projective test. The narrative was of another boy with a small penis who had told me that he sometimes wondered if God had really intended for him to be a girl—in fact, he once had a dream in which he actually turned into a girl. The boy's response to this narrative was that he himself had thought of changing to a girl. This was the point I switched on the tape recorder. [The transcript is as follows, with the interviewer's questions and comments in italic and the boy's answers in regular type.]

I asked you if you ever had the feeling that you would like to be a girl.

Yes, I would like to be a girl, but I wouldn't like to do the things that a girl does. I'd like to be born a girl.

You had better explain that some more to me.

I'd like to be doing the things that a boy does....Well, I would like to be born a girl—but I might want to do most of the things that a girl does.

Why would you like to be born a girl?

Oh, because you can have a baby. You could have a baby and take care of it. And that would be fun when it was a little child, you know. You would play with it sometimes when you are around with it. But, probably, getting it to sleep wouldn't be too much fun. Because sometimes it's harder to get babies to sleep.

A father can play with a baby and put it to sleep and everything.

Yes, I know that.... I would rather be doing what a mother does. I've seen my mother do the things. I like the things like ironing clothes and washing, and it's fun. I've ironed clothes a lot for my mother. And I take them off the line when they are dry and when they are coming out of the washing machine, you know. And, it would just be fun to be a little girl.

When did you first figure out that you would like to be a girl?

A long time ago. I wanted to be a girl ever since I wished to be a girl.

How long is a long time ago?

A year or so. I kept on wishing that I was a girl.

You said that you would like to have a baby. How much do you know about where babies come from?

The sperm. That's where they come from.

Where does the sperm come from?

The father. But I probably wouldn't have a sperm. So why be a boy if you can't have a sperm and your penis is small?

[There then ensued an explanation of donor insemination and the sperm bank, and a lengthy conversation on how sperms get out of the penis. He was uncertain as to whether his own penis had ever become erect, and whether he had good feelings in it. Then the talk turned to pregnancy, and the way that the baby comes through the vagina, the same place where the penis goes. Reflecting on this information, he then went on:] I would like to be a girl, and I would like to have a baby. I wouldn't like very much carrying it around, you know. I only would like to be a girl. I don't know anything else to say about it.

Have you found a boyfriend yet?

What do you mean?

If you are a girl, and are going to have a baby, you have a boyfriend and then a husband.

Well, I'm not a girl. I haven't got a boyfriend. But if I was a girl, I could find a boyfriend. There's a lot of boys in college. You can go to college. You can find a lot of boyfriends. That's how my father found a wife.

You are not in love then, yet?

No; well, I have two girls that I love.

Do you ever have any thoughts in your mind about being able to have a baby, but the way a father has one?

Yeah. I thought that I could have a baby, you know, if I had a different penis. I don't know how the sperms could get up there, you know. I know that there was some fluid that sperms would swim in, and to go up. I couldn't do it. The sperms just went up, but I don't know how...they came out, because you just can't make a sperm come out like that....

I wonder how you would feel if you could get some size to your penis.

Well, I wouldn't want to be a girl any more. Because, if I had a penis big enough to have sperm, I would like to have the sperm to put it up the vagina.

[The interviewer then outlined two hypothetical treatment options, masculine and feminine, neither totally satisfactory, and both without fertility, and asked if the decision between them would be difficult. The boy replied:]

No, I want to be a boy. I would like to be the man. If you have to pay all that money just for an operation so you can have a vagina, and I would think to look like a girl, and can't get a baby out of you, what's the use of wasting all that money—if you have to go and get another baby?"

Supplied with information about the use of testosterone ointment to give an immediate boost in penis size, he had no hesitation in opting to try it, while leaving open the option of reconsidering being a girl. In further conversation about the origin of his idea of changing sex, he said that he had read some media references to Christine Jorgensen (1967), the transsexual whose story had first astonished the world several years earlier.

─── 15 ───

Lovemap Development

Everyone has a personal lovemap encoded synchronously in the mind/brain regardless of sexological disability (Money, 1986a/1993). A lovemap is as personalized as one's face, fingerprint, or speaking voice, even though its contents, like an individual's native language, are in part widely shared. The lovemap may be likened to a personalized mental videotape or movie, in which the star performer has all of the qualities that fit one's ideally perfect lover and erotic partner. This mental movie also features all of the activities of the ideally perfect love affair and its erotic consummation. The lovemap may also be activated with a live partner(s) in performances that match the ideal either perfectly or with some degree of compromise.

Lovemaps are gender coded as homosexual, heterosexual, or as bisexual. Lovemaps are coded on a continuum between hyposexual and hypersexual and also coded on a continuum of normophilic and paraphilic (kinky). A lovemap is not finished and in place at birth but, like a language, develops during infancy and childhood. Although a lovemap is definitively shaped before puberty, it is with the hormonal influx of puberty that it fully reveals itself. Projections of the lovemap appear spontaneously in romantic and sexually explicit erotic imagery and ideas in reveries, fantasies, masturbation fantasies, dreams, and wet dreams.

When two people are romantically and erotically attracted to one another, the more perfect the reciprocal matching of the two lovemaps, the more wondrous their relationship and, by and large, the more long-lasting. Conversely, the less the lovemaps of the two individuals match, the greater the fragility of the relationship. If the mismatch is two-sided, then the partners can separate without the difficulties of a one-sided attraction. "Fatal attraction" is the term popularly used when two lovemaps collide. One person wrongly decodes the lovemap of the other as being a suitable match and locks onto it, and then the lock freezes. This unilateral fixation on unrequited love is identified as the Clérambault-Kandinsky syndrome, named for the two French physicians who wrote about it. Formerly, it was known also as erotomania. An example of the syndrome is personified in John Hinckley, who attempted to assassinate then-President Ronald Reagan in a desperate attempt to publicly declare his unrequited love for the actress Jodie Foster. Many people with the syndrome stalk the recipient of their one-sided love, and they may become homicidal as well as suicidal. Love is an agony as well as an ecstasy.

Two lovemaps may mismatch on gender coding, if one is bisexual and the other exclusively heterosexual or homosexual, or if one is homosexual and the other heterosexual. Mismatching obviously can occur with individual coordinates on the continuum of hyposexual or hypersexual intensity. Mismatching can also occur when one lovemap is kinky or paraphilic in a way that the other lovemap is not. Two distinct paraphilias will also constitute a mismatch.

There are two criteria of a normophilic lovemap: statistical and ideological. Statistically normophilic means being not at the extremes but among the 50% who belong in the middle group of the distribution (i.e., those who are average). Ideologically normophilic means being conformist or orthodox with respect to sexual imagery, ideation, and practice and being obedient to the rules or admonitions of authorities. With respect to their sexuality or any other characteristic, most people when they ask, "Am I normal?" mean "Am I acceptable and do I meet with your approval?"

When a lovemap is normophilic, it may also be construed as being neither hyposexual nor hypersexual. The opposite of the continuum of normophilic, however, is usually construed as being paraphilic (from the Greek *para-*, altered and *-philia*, love). Heterosexual, bisexual, or homosexual lovemaps may be paraphilic, although they are more usually normophilic.

The criterion of a paraphilic lovemap is that it does not conform to someone else's, and possibly also to one's own, expectations, rules, or laws of what is sexually orthodox, approved, or permitted. Paraphilia, when it occurs in females, is likely to be associated with tactile imagery and ideation. In males, by contrast, paraphilic imagery and ideation are more likely to be visual. At one extreme, some paraphilias are harmless and playful, and at the other extreme, some are injurious and deadly. An example is bondage and discipline (B & D), which is classified as a subvariety of sadomasochism (S/M). Light bondage and discipline may be considered playful and harmless, although not by everyone, whereas heavy

B & D may entail major bodily injury and, even when consensual, may be fatal. If two lovemaps are mismatched for bondage and discipline, however, the partner whose lovemap lacks a B & D component either is blatantly turned off by such activity or fakes its erotic appeal. Faking of erotic interest stresses any relationship.

According to evidence presently available, when healthy lovemap development is impaired, the outcome typically results in a split between romantic love and carnal lust. In such a lovemap, love is encoded above the belt while lust is encoded below the belt. Love is romantic and affiliative. Lust is carnal and orgastic. Love may be publicly expressed and admired. Lust is publicly repressed and judged obscene.

In girls with a lovemap impaired in this way, the outcome of the split between love and lust is likely to be that romantic love remains intact, whereas carnal lust becomes shut down or dormant.

In boys with such an impaired lovemap, it is more likely that love and lust will each continue to be active but separately. Instead of being unified with love, lust becomes diverted and detoured into an alternative, paraphilic route of expression. For example, an 8-year-old boy who is abusively punished for proudly exhibiting his penis to his girlfriend might subsequently become compulsively fixated on exhibiting his penis in lust for strangers whom he does not love, while at the same time being unable to become aroused by lust for the wife whom he does love. Proverbially, there has been for males a separation between the whore and the madonna and, for females, between the playboy and the provider.

When a lovemap does not develop in a normophilic way in childhood, it may be characterized as warped, distorted, or vandalized (Money & Lamacz, 1989). Sexological health is not automatically guaranteed in childhood but, like all aspects of pediatric health, needs adequate attention and care. Usually, however, it is neglected. There are no sexual health clinics in children's hospitals and, amazingly enough, none for adolescents. Impairments and defects of lovemap development are, therefore, usually overlooked in the early stages before they become too firmly imprinted and resistant to change in adolescence and adulthood.

The sources of lovemap impairments may be identifiably related to the mismanagement of genital self-play in infancy and to the mismanagement of age-mate sexual rehearsal play later in childhood. As mentioned earlier, such play is normally encountered not only in humans, but other primates as well. Rehearsal play, along with sexual learning, may be subject to deprivation and neglect. More likely, sexual rehearsal play will be subject to abusive punishment and humiliation by parents and other adults who misguidedly impair the very normality that they want in their children's lovemaps.

When children are prematurely engaged in sexual rehearsal play that is out of synchrony with their developmental ages, healthy lovemap development may also be impaired. The risk of such impairment increases if there is coercion, if there is too great of an age discrepancy between the participants, and if bodily abuse and injury are inflicted. The greatest damage, however, comes from the dilemma of an individual's being "damned if you do and damned if you don't" get discovered or report whatever sexual exploration that has been happening. Entrapment in this dilemma is the penalty exacted by the powerful and all-pervasive sexual taboo, which demands secrecy and deceit.

Impairment of lovemap development may be a sequel to diverse traumas and stresses that may not be explicitly sexual. A history of abuse, neglect, and deprivation in childhood of the type that produces the retarded physical, intellectual, and social maturation of the Kaspar Hauser syndrome also produces vandalization of the lovemap (Money, 1992).

In children with a sex error or other sexological condition, especially one that involves long-term intervention, regular clinic visits, and frequent hospitalizations, particularly for genital surgery, lovemap development may become impaired. To prevent or minimize the development of such impairment, sexological health care needs to become a component of general pediatric and adolescent (ephebiatric) health care. To neglect sexological health care for children with a history of sex error of the body and to ignore ongoing impairment in their developing lovemaps amounts to de facto malpractice.

Conclusion

It is probably a good idea for all young people to have a brief acquaintance, in the course of their sexological education, with the fact that genetic defects could cross their own paths, with the fact that some of them may experience impairment of sexological function, and with the possibility that anomalies of sex may occur in the newborn and growing child. Forewarned is forearmed. Knowledge is prophylactic, whether in its applicability to oneself or to one's community of relatives and friends. Every young person will eventually hear or know of at least one individual with one of the anomalies mentioned in this book. Moreover, although they do not need to hear the voice of a prophet of doom, young people develop in wisdom if they hear at least once that the exuberance of romance and the ecstasy of love and sex are not only a resolution of adolescent yearning or distress, but also the beginning of the presentation of fresh challenges to oneself, of unknown demands of fate, and of a new dimension of life to master.

References

Allen, L.S., & Gorski, R.A. (1992). Sexual orientation and the size of the anterior commissure in the human brain. *Proceedings of the National Academy of Sciences, USA, 89,* 7199–7202.

American Psychiatric Association. (1994). *Diagnostic and statistical manual of mental disorders* (4th ed.). Washington, DC: Author.

Bick, D., Franco, B., Sherins, R.J., Heye, B., Pike, L., Crawford, J., Maddalena, A., Incerti, B., Pragliola, A., Meitinger, T., & Ballabio, A. (1992). Brief report: Intragenic deletion of the KALIG-1 gene in Kallmann's syndrome. *New England Journal of Medicine, 326,* 1752–1755.

Clarke, I.J. (1977). The sexual behavior of prenatally androgenized ewes observed in the field. *Journal of Reproduction and Fertility, 49,* 311–315.

Dorland's Illustrated Medical Dictionary (26th ed.). (1981). Philadelphia: W.B. Saunders.

Fausto-Sterling, A. (1993). The five sexes: Why male and female are not enough. *The Sciences, 33*(3), 20–24.

Green, R. (1986). *"The sissy boy syndrome" and the development of homosexuality.* New Haven: Yale University Press.

Hamer, D.H., Hu, S., Magnuson, V.L., Hu, N., & Pattatucci, A.M.L. (1993). A linkage between DNA markers on the X chromosome and male sexual orientation. *Science, 261,* 321–327.

Herdt, G.H., & Davidson, J. (1988). The Sambia "turnim-man": Sociocultural and clinical aspects of gender formation in male pseudohermaphrodites with 5-alpha-reductase deficiency in Papua New Guinea. *Archives of Sexual Behavior, 17,* 33–56.

Imperato-McGinley, J., Guerrero, L., Gautier, T., & Peterson, R.E. (1974). Steroid 5α-reductase deficiency in man: An inherited form of male pseudohermaphroditism. *Science, 186,* 1213–1215.

Imperato-McGinley, J., Peterson, R.E., Gautier, T., & Sturla, E. (1979). Androgen and the evolution of male-gender identity among male pseudohermaphrodites with 5α-reductase deficiency. *New England Journal of Medicine, 300,* 1233–1237.

Jacobs, P.A., Brunton, M., Melville, M.M., Brittain, R.P., & McClemont, W.F. (1965). Aggressive behavior, mental sub-normality and the XYY male. *Nature, 208,* 1351–1352.

Jackson, P., Barrowclough, I.W., France, J.T., & Phillips, L.I. (1980). A successful pregnancy following total hysterectomy. *British Journal of Obstetrics and Gynaecology, 87,* 353–355.

Jorgensen, C. (1967). *Christine Jorgensen: A personal autobiography.* New York: Paul S. Eriksson.

Klebs, E. (1876). *Handbuch der pathologischen anatomie* [Handbook of pathological anatomy]. Berlin: A. Herschwald.

LeVay, S. (1991). A difference in hypothalamic structure between heterosexual and homosexual men. *Science, 253,* 1034–1037.

Lightfoot-Klein, H. (1989). *Prisoners of ritual: An odyssey into female genital circumcision in Africa.* Binghamton, NY: Haworth Press.

Michael, R.P., & Zumpe, D. (1993). Medroxyprogesterone acetate decreases the sexual activity of male cynomolgus monkeys *(Macaca fascicularis):* An action on the brain? *Physiology & Behavior, 53,* 783–788.

Migeon, C.J., & Forest, M.G. (1983). Androgens in biological fluids. In B. Rothfield (Ed.), *Nuclear medicine in vitro* (2nd ed., pp. 145–170). Philadelphia: J.B. Lippincott.

Money, J. (1968). *Sex errors of the body: Dilemmas, education, counseling.* Baltimore: The Johns Hopkins University Press.

Money, J. (1986a/1993). *Lovemaps: Clinical concepts of sexual/erotic health and pathology, paraphilia, and gender transposition in childhood, adolescence, and maturity.* Buffalo, NY: Prometheus Books.

Money, J. (1986b). *Venuses penuses: Sexology, sexosophy, and exigency theory.* Buffalo, NY: Prometheus Books.

Money, J. (1987). Psychologic considerations in patients with ambisexual development. *Seminars in Reproductive Endocrinology, 5,* 307–313.

Money, J. (1991). *Biographies of gender and hermaphroditism in paired comparisons: Clinical supplement to the handbook of sexology.* Amsterdam: Elsevier.

Money, J. (1992). *The Kaspar Hauser syndrome of "psychosocial dwarfism:" Deficient statural, intellectual, and social growth induced by child abuse.* Buffalo, NY: Prometheus Books.

Money, J. (1994a). Hormones, hormonal anomalies, and psychologic healthcare. In M.S. Kappy, R.M. Blizzard, & C.J. Migeon (Eds.), *Wilkins' diagnosis and treatment of endocrine disorders in childhood and adolescence* (4th ed., pp. 1141–1178). Springfield, IL: Charles C Thomas.

Money, J. (1994b). *Reinterpreting the unspeakable: Human sexuality 2000—The complete interviewer and clinical biographer, exigency theory, and sexology for the third millenium.* New York: Continuum Press.

Money, J., & Lamacz, M. (1989). *Vandalized lovemaps: Paraphilic outcome of seven cases in pediatric sexology.* Buffalo, NY: Prometheus Books.

Money, J., & Norman, B.F. (1988). Pedagogical handicap associated with micropenis and other CHARGE syndrome anomalies of embryogenesis: Four 46XY cases reared as girls. *American Journal of Psychotherapy, 42,* 354–379.

Money, J., & Pranzarone, G.F. (1993). Development of paraphilia in childhood and adolescence. *Child and Adolescent Psychiatric Clinics of North America, 2,* 463–475.

Money, J., & Russo, A.J. (1979). Homosexual outcome of discordant gender-identity/role in childhood: Longitudinal follow-up. *Journal of Pediatric Psychology, 4,* 29–41.

Pang, S.Y., Wallace, M.A., & Thuline, H.C. (1988). Worldwide experience in newborn screening for classical congenital adrenal hyperplasia due to 21-hydroxylase deficiency. *Pediatrics, 81,* 866–874.

Rees, H.D., Bonsall, R.W., & Michael, R.P. (1986). Preoptic and hypothalamic neurons accumulate [^{3}H]medroxyprogesterone acetate in male cynomolgus monkeys. *Life Sciences, 39,* 1353–1359.

Short, R.V., & Clarke, I.J. (n.d.). *Masculinization of the female sheep.* (Distributed by MRC Reproductive Biology Unit, 2 Forrest Road, Edinburgh, EHI 2QW, U.K.)

Swaab, D.F., & Hofman, M.A. (1990). An enlarged suprachiasmatic nucleus in homosexual men. *Brain Research, 537,* 141–148.

Tijo, J.H., & Levan, A. (1956). The chromosome number of man. *Hereditas, 42,* 1–6.

Wilson, C.A., Gonzales, I., & Farabollini, F. (1991). Behavioral effects in adulthood of neonatal manipulation of brain serotonin levels in normal and androgenized females. *Pharmacology Biochemistry and Behavior, 41,* 91–98.

Wilson, C.A., Pearson, J.A., Hunter, A.J., Tuohy, P.A., & Payne, A.P. (1986). The effect of neonatal manipulation of hypothalamic serotonin levels on sexual activity in the adult rat. *Pharmacology Biochemistry and Behavior, 24,* 1175–1183.

Index